Clouds Like Horses
and Other Stories

Stephanie Hart

First paperback trade edition 2009

Designed by Laywan Kwan

All rights reserved, including the
right to reproduce this book or portions
thereof in any form whatsoever. For
information contact Stephanie Hart at
stephanie700@aol.com

Copyright © 2009 by Stephanie Hart
ISBN: 978-0-578-00933-9

for Robert Roth

and the memory of my mother

and father

Table of Contents

Acknowledgements
Author's Note

I	*Childhood by the Sea*	1
II	*The Boarding School Years*	37
III	*High School and Beyond*	72
IV	*Family History*	115
V	*Coming to Terms*	165

Acknowledgements

I want to thank the editors of *And Then, ducts.org* and *The Sun*, where a number of these stories first appeared. "Making Music," "Without Warning," and a version of "Visiting Keats Urn" appeared in *And Then*. "In the Middle of the Night," "Waking Up," "Getting Ready," and "Parties" appeared in *The Sun*. "Mona Lisa Smile," "Bound for Greatness," and "A Walk with my Father," were derived from and inspired by my essay, "A Letter to My Father on the Tenth Anniversary of his Death," which appeared in *ducts.org* and is included in the anthology, *How to Greet Famous People: The Best Stories from ducts.org*, published by Green Point Press and edited by Jonathan Kravetz and Charles Salzberg. I want to extend a special thanks to both of them.

I want to thank Nancy Aronie for inviting me to read the story, "Dinner at Our House," on her radio show, *Writing from the Heart*. I want to thank Robert Roth, co-creator of *And Then*, for inviting me to read, "Sailing," on the radio broadcast, *Words on Wings*.

★ ★ ★

Many people have been instrumental in making this book a reality.

I want to begin by thanking Laywan Kwan and Thitirut Sutjaritmaneekul for the superb book design and graphics.

I want to thank Memory Keeper Photo as well as Chris Quarksnow for their fine work with Photoshop.

I want to thank Shelley Haven for her magnificent cover photograph.

I want to thank Jane Gill for her exquisite photographs, which elucidate a number of the stories.

I want to thank my good friend, Barbara Johnson, for providing a photograph of us as children and for her enduring confidence in me.

I want to extend heartfelt thanks to Regina McBride for her invaluable editorial suggestions and for her workshop, Inner Lives, in which many of these stories were written. I want to thank Regina and the other members of the group for their astute and intuitive comments.

I want to thank Janice Eidus for her sound advice and her enthusiasm for this project.

I want to thank Thaddeus Rutkowski for his insightful editing of the story, "Snapshots."

I want to create a sacred circle of thanks for Nancy Aronie. In her workshop, Writing from the Heart, I was able to unearth what was deepest and most significant in myself and find a frame for it in words. Many of the stories were written in her circle.

I want to thank Candace Reid, Kathleen DeFoux, and Heather Andrade, my writing circle of friends, whose loving energy infiltrates every page.

I want to thank Marilyn Graman for her inspiring teaching. Her unique take on life has become part of the fabric of my writing and thinking.

I want to thank my dear friend, Linda Wilhelm, for her belief in and appreciation of my writing. I want to thank Janice Eidus, John Kastan, Alma Kastan, Alexandra Leaf, Sylvia Wertheimer, Sharyn Finkelstein, Karen Ogulnick, Oliver Ogulnick, Elise Hurley, Enid Gold, Shelley Haven, Fran Nesi, Dave Neiditch, Marguerite Z. Bunyan, Rosemarie Ottomanelli, Monique Simón and all my friends at FIT for their support and encouragement during the writing process.

And last but not least I want to thank Robert Roth for strongly suggesting that these stories be developed into a book.

Author's Note

The people and events I've written about are substantially real and true. Yet, this book is not a memoir in the strictest sense. I have changed names, dates, in some instances, facts. The vignettes about my ancestors in Russia are inspired by a felt sense of their characters and personalities.

I have arranged the stories in a loose chronology. They flow together and are informed by memory and imagination. Each story has its own rhythm and intention. I invite you to listen.

Stephanie Hart

August 2008

PART I

Childhood by the Sea

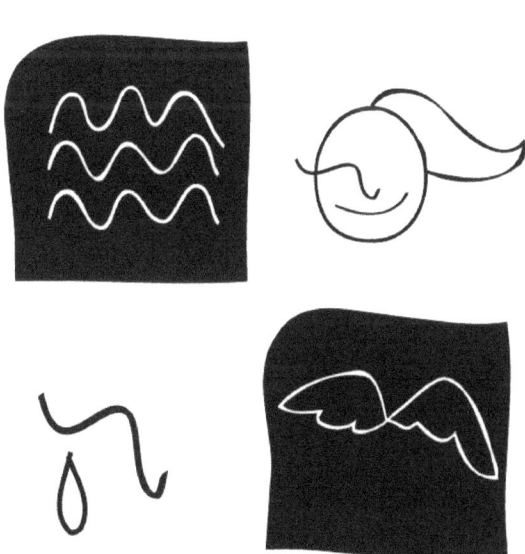

Dinner at our House

I can't remember a family dinner at our house by the sea. I know that my mother, my father, and I were there. And I was small. I may have been wearing red corduroy trousers and a ponytail. Beyond the window the ocean looked vast and cold. I could see pirate ships bouncing on the horizon.

The dining table sat against a wall in the living room; there may have been plates and napkins on it. It is the chill and shadow of a skylight that I remember, and the width of the room, and the wind that could have carried us all out to sea. My father chews noisily and wipes his face with the back of his hand. My mother, who is more genteel, embroiders smoke rings in the air; her brown hair is tied back in a scarf; she isn't smiling. My father smirks and dips his wide chin. "You can't trust anyone," he says. My mother butters a roll and returns it to her plate. She turns to me. I look at the sea. There are crayoned chimneys dancing in the sky; white sails touch heads and stand back up again. The sea and the sky become one world one sound—Help; get me out of here!

Darkness comes. The curtains draw themselves, or my mother

draws them. Plates disappear. The distance between the table and my room feels like a continent of linoleum. My father, lost in the silence of contempt, doesn't notice me. My mother laughs; her eyes dance in her thin cheeks, and I hear the wind over her voice. I follow it to my room with its red speckled floor. I am hungry for something other than dinner. In the depth of my bed I imagine the darkness—a chocolate cake of sorrow. I take a bite and roll over on my stomach. I press my foot against the blue wall and feel the dimensions of my body. What if the darkness could envelop me like syrup, and I could sail away on the sweet sticky awe of the night?

The Bed

I love the narrow bed that stands against the blue wall in my room. It is a little longer and wider than I am and has a cherry-red quilt. I am six. At night I lie on my back and make stars appear on the ceiling: big white stars that glow in the dark and a moon that is fat and round and white and has lips and a nose and eyes. It is the time before sleep that I like best. I run my fingers along the satin rim of my blanket. I find a soft place in the mattress for the small of my back. I feel safe and comfortable. My mother's red mouth can't shout at me. She can't threaten to give all my toys away to some other little girl. My father's thick chin can't bob up and down as he tells me how stupid I sound when I count in French. And the black dog in my storybook with the patch over one eye can't sneak out of the pages of the book and frighten me.

When I walk on tiptoe during the day, I usually trip. At night I see myself as a prima ballerina in a white tutu and pink satin slippers. I take graceful steps. I leap and pirouette. I turn the bed into a trampoline.

One night I invite Peter Pan to join me, and he accepts. He calls me Sonia, the dancing princess. I call him Pete. He has a blond cowlick and blue eyes that twinkle. We jump off the bed high into the air that becomes the sky; we soar over chimneys and buildings that have lighted windows. Pete offers to take me to Neverland, but I decline. I'd like to meet the Lost Boys and the Indians, but I'm not about to risk being chased by Captain Hook.

I lead the way to a land where the grass is a new shade of green and wild flowers can talk and sing. They tell us to visit the king and queen in their tree house. The queen recognizes us right away and serves us chocolate milk. The king pulls on his mustache and smiles. "This is the land of truth," the queen says. "Everyone here is nice to one another, and we eat biscuits."

Pete and I climb to the top of the tallest tree with the other children. The clouds brush our cheeks. We can see the ocean beneath us. We dive into the sea and ride on the backs of waves. Suddenly the water gets calm and the sky dark. My eyelids are heavy. I am on my bed on soft pink sheets under the stars.

Mimi Freeman

The summer I turned seven my neighbor, Mimi Freeman, dyed her hair pink and ran off to join a Calypso band. "It's a scandal," my mother said. Mimi's husband, Jim, and her son, Pete, would have to pack up their things, sell their house, and leave the neighborhood.

Mimi and I had been great friends before her sudden departure. If she noticed I was a kid, she never let on. She lived in a large white house with lots of windows right across the street from the blue ranch house where I lived with my parents. Both houses faced the sea. There was nothing I liked better than visiting Mimi. I loved her slightly buck teeth and her long dangling earrings. Her hair was blond then, almost like the sun. Her skirts were long and flowing.

"Come in," Mimi would say. "I have some strawberry milk for us today. It's delicious." We would sit together on her white sofa and take sips. We ate cookies that tasted better than anything. The rest of her house was white too: clean and fresh as if it were waiting to be entered.

Mimi and I went exploring. I remember the first time she led me up the two flights of stairs that stopped in front of a small white door. It creaked when she opened it. The room inside was low and narrow and almost empty except for a few paintings on the floor leaning up against a wall; they were of apples and pears and grapes that looked real enough to bite into.

"Shush," Mimi said, putting a finger to her lips even though I hadn't said anything. "Let the colors speak to us." After a while they did. Red sounded like a drum. Yellow like kites flying; green like the rush of water.

It wasn't long before Mimi urged me to look for myself. Her blue eyes were clear and bright. "Go ahead," she said. "See what you can find." I felt a quickening of excitement as I walked up the stairs.

After Mimi left, I found colors and shapes everywhere, even in the darkness. When I saw a rabbit hop across my yard, I felt she was watching it with me. I haven't seen my neighbor, Mimi Freeman, since that summer, yet when the sun burns outside my window at dusk in August, and each time I see beauty in art and nature, I hear her voice, which has become my voice too, "What do you see? What do you hear?"

Praying

My parents were renegade Jews when it came to the rituals of prayers. God's name was never mentioned in our house except in vain. "Oh, God," my mother would say. "Where are my cigarettes?"

My friend Eileen went to church every Sunday and said her prayers every night. She had so many things to thank God for: her doll Maryanne with the brown wavy hair, the way the rain sounded outside her window, her brother John and her fuzzy pink slippers.

In first grade Eileen and I sat at adjoining desks and a girl named Lucy sat in front of us. I liked her long, shiny, blond hair and her eyes, which couldn't quite decide on their color. She had a doll named Genevieve with yellow braids that was almost always with her. Lucy had four brothers, Pete, Jeff, Ralph, and Joe. Pete, the oldest, would walk Lucy home from school to their two-story house on Darlington Road; he could hit a baseball so far and so fast that it made my head spin when I watched him. Lucy's mother, who volunteered in the schoolyard, had red hair and freckles and could jump rope better than any kid. Her father whose name was Charles traveled all over the country for business. When he came home from a trip to Minnesota, he found that his house had burned to the ground and Lucy and her mother and her four brothers with it.

Our teacher, Mrs. Walsh, told us to say a prayer for Lucy. And so one night in my room with only a rabbit watching on the other side of the glass door I began, "Dear God," I said. "Make sure Lucy is having fun in heaven. Don't let her be afraid. I hope she has her doll Genevieve with her."

I tried praying again the next night. This time I asked God to take good care of my mother and father, not the mother who threatened to give my dolls away to some other little girl and laughed when I cried, or the father who taunted me when I couldn't count perfectly in French, but the parents who came into my room to say good night and smiled gently into the darkness. I blessed the rabbit in my yard with the scary red eyes and the Dalmatian, Queenie, next door, who chased me around our backyard, and his owner Mimi Freeman, who wrapped her hair in a pink turban and splashed swirls of color on a white canvass. I prayed for my best friend Johnny C, who had a cowlick and shiny brown eyes and a birthmark on his left check.

At school when the kids teased me because my mother dressed me in embroidered smocks, and my hair was a bush of corkscrew curls, I was determined to ask God to make me beautiful and smart. But when the world turned dark and the sounds of the night came into my room like whispers from the sky, and I felt a warm familiar hum in my chest, I began to bless everyone I knew.

Good Mother Bad Mother

"Who scribbled those lines on the wall?" my father wants to know.

I have painted my own rendition of the sun in burnt orange crayon above my bed. Dark squiggly lines disrupt the calm blue paint. I am five.

"Who did it?" he shouts.

"Not me," I say. My voice comes out cracked and small like Pooh Bear's when he is stuck in a tunnel. "I didn't do it. It was Greenie."

Greenie is my imaginary friend. She has a complexion the color of lime green Jell-O and a skein of silky green hair unlike my dark corkscrew curls. I don't mind blaming her because she can run away faster than I can.

Dad leans toward me like a big, angry grizzly bear. "Admit what you did!"

I feel myself shrinking, becoming small and hollow like a rag doll without the stuffing. It is not Greenie but my mother who comes to my rescue. "That's enough, Lou. She's only a little girl."

I watch my mother glide across the speckled floor of my room in a long blue skirt. Her peasant blouse falls over her shoulders. There are flecks of red in her long, auburn hair. How could anyone be more beautiful? My mother comes over to me and enfolds me in her arms. I smell tobacco on her fingertips and perfume on her wrists. My body takes on her scent and texture. My head finds the pillow of her stomach. "You're a part of me," she says. "I won't let Daddy yell at you anymore."

That night my mother comes into my room and snuggles up next to me. I tangle my short stubby legs with her longer ones, knitting us together. "I know you drew that picture and not Greenie," my mother says. "I won't tell Daddy."

"I know," I say.

We sing lullabies in Yiddish and in English. My mother's voice, which sounds more like talking than singing, is sort of loud and off key; mine is soft and sweet. "You're my beautiful, wonderful, smart little girl," she says when we finish. I fall into a fuzzy kind of sleep, rocked by her presence and the darkness.

The sun is shining. I am climbing the steel ladder to my lookout tower while my mother watches. Once on top I look at the sky and the trees. I hear a robin's nest whisper. My mother calls up to me, "Hold on for God's sake. You'll fall on your face. Stupid, ugly girl." My legs turn to liquid. I grip the bars tightly to steady myself. The sky becomes an underwater painting through my tears.

When I wolf down Cheerios and milk from my Alice in Wonderland bowl, so I can see the white rabbit at the bottom, she sneers at me. "You're a little pig, aren't you?" Tears that burn like soot well up in my eyes; my chest is hot and tight. Since she won't go away, I crawl into my invisible turtle shell where it is soft and moist and dark and nobody can see in, but I can see out. Sometimes when I look in the mirror, I see what my mother sees. I want to hide that fat, stupid, ugly little girl away from everyone.

Clouds like Horses

We are in my mother's bedroom where the big standing fan tries to make a breeze. My mother and I lie shoulder-to-shoulder on my parent's king-size-bed. Beyond the bed there is a picture window. I can see white clouds like horses' footprints moving in the distance.

Today my mother is wearing a dotted Swiss blouse and a white cotton skirt. She has her feet up on the bed, and her sandals look like wedges of cake. She is making me a necklace for my seventh birthday. She rolls tiny white ivory beads onto a piece of wire. Before I know it the beads are on the string and around my neck fastened with a tiny ivory clasp.

"There," my mother says. "For my precious little girl. You have such a sweet voice just like my own mother, Sonia, your grandmother. She died when I was fourteen. I remember the morning perfectly. The house was quiet except for the ticking of the grandfather clock in the foyer. Then there was a thud; my papa came running; it was Sunday. He was reading the newspaper in the kitchen. His glasses fell off and broke into pieces. My sister Rose had on a white hat with a wide brim. She was shouting, 'Help us.' Mama looked like she was asleep when I saw her; she was so still."

Sometimes when my mother tells this story, the grandfather clock isn't ticking; sometimes her sister Rose has on a red hat and her papa's glasses don't break. But her mother always falls to the floor and never gets up again.

My mother puts her arms around me. Her perfume smells like rose petals. I hug her back, putting my chin on her shoulder.

"Don't ever leave me, sweetheart," she says.

"I won't, Mommy. I promise," I say, watching the clouds. The footprints are farther in the distance. The horses are running like no one can stop them.

Snapshots

My mother's laughter cuts right through me. I am five in a white organdy dress with a green sash. Moving my arms up and down, I tiptoe across the living room on my Mary Janes. The floor has a slippery, sliding feeling. I trip into a puddle of organdy. My mother moves toward me. "You're a clumsy little girl, aren't you?" I see her slanted green cat's eyes and her pink nails like tiny claws. She wipes a smudge off my cheek; her thumb pokes at me like an elf that says, "I hate you." I close my eyes, hoping that she will disappear or I will. We don't. I make myself get up. I spin away from her, moving faster and faster, but I can't escape her. Her eyes are everywhere and they burn my skin.

There are gentler windows on my childhood I can open. I see the ocean in sunshine. I feel salty spray. I am running along the shoreline laughing as if the sound of the sea were inside me.

"Got you, sweetheart," my mother says, coming up behind me. She throws a big yellow towel around me. I smell her sweet, grimy wet bathing suit. I look up at her. Her chestnut-colored hair falls to her shoulders. She has red lips and smooth white cheeks. "You're my beautiful little girl," she says.

I see blue sky and tall buildings. I am eight. My mother and I are walking down a Manhattan street. She smells of morning air and sweet perfume. She has colored her hair in many shades of blond. I see streaks of gold in it. She takes my arm; the skin of her wrist is soft to the touch. Around us big yellow cabs with swivel seats inside them whiz up Madison Avenue.

We keep walking. The pavement is smooth under my feet.

"Can we stop at Schraffts for peanut butter and jelly sandwiches?" I ask after a while.

"Sure baby doll. Of course we can." Her voice sounds like music.

"Let's go to Woolworth's for ice cream after. I want a vanilla cone with pineapple and chocolate sprinkles."

She laughs. "You can have anything you want today, honey."

My mother is almost marching she is so happy. She is in love with herself, Manhattan, and me.

We climb up the winding staircase to her apartment on Lexington Avenue. I love the thick gray carpet and the twin beds covered in gold brocade to make them look like couches. Tall gold lamps that curve like Egyptian statues stand on either side of the room. My mother got them in a thrift shop on Third Avenue. She says they have magical powers. I think so too. My parents are separated. My mother lives on the east side of Central Park and my father on the west. I live in a boarding school in Northern New Jersey. I am home for Easter vacation.

My mother and me, 1961

My mother takes out her sewing box. She is making satin pillows for my GiGi doll. GiGi has pink hair and a body that feels like real skin; the doll has a button nose like mine. I sit down next to my mother and watch her. She is intent on each stitch, casting it like golden thread in a fairytale. She hands me the tiny satin pillows when they are finished. They are a pale pink color like the inside of a shell and softer than anything. I press them against my cheeks.

I have on a yellow cotton skirt and a soft yellow sweater. My mother and I are sitting opposite each other in the cream-colored kitchen of the Brooklyn apartment she shares with my stepfather, where I visit them on weekends and holidays. A globe light made of red, green, and blue plastic hangs above us, catching the light from the window. My mother claps her hands together. "That's wonderful, sweetheart. Read it again, please, just for me." It is my sixth grade essay about shadows. I tell how they look like lassos and mountains and clouds and how they are only scary if you think they are. "Bravo," my mother applauds. The warmth of her smile ignites a smile on my lips. I feel everything is shining.

Time seems less relevant than the feelings that bind my mother and me. Thirty years later we are in Florida, and she is dying. She wraps her thin arms around my waist, and I hug her back. I stroke the nape of her neck. She is birdlike and tender. I hold her rage, her concealed guilt as well as her love. She senses my good will. "God bless you," she says.

My mother has been dead for five years, and at times I wonder if she ever existed. My self-hating voice reminds me that she did. And another voice, the one that urges me to walk through fear and uncertainty, also has her echo. I want to gather up these voices and tell her story and mine.

The 1930 census gives me definitive proof of her life. I find my grandfather Joseph Tolchinsky, a Russian immigrant living in Newark, New Jersey with his wife, Sonia, his daughter, Ada, his son Nathan and his youngest daughter, Gertrude, my mother then nine years old. I imagine her in a starched white jumper and white shoes. Her brown hair is cut close to her head in bangs. She points her chin at a window. I feel anger rear up from the coils of fear inside her. Can I listen?

The Gun

When my mother was nine, she accidentally shot herself in the thigh. She discovered a .22 caliber semiautomatic pistol in a bureau in her house in Newark. Her brother Nathan, who was nineteen and purported to have underworld connections, kept the gun for protection. My mother never intended to fire it; she fingered the barrel and the trigger. She ran her hand along the cold muzzle. She lifted the gun, pretending to take aim when her hand slipped and hit the trigger. The pain of the bullet was as fierce as the sound of the gun firing; she was sure she was dying. Her mother ran to her from the kitchen with a look of horror on her face.

The ambulance came and whisked my mother to the hospital. When she came up from the ether, her mama and papa were watching her. Her brother Nathan had his lips in a snarl; he was sure she would die just to spite him. Her older sister, Ada, looked frightened and amazed. My mother tried to smile at all of them. She was alive after all. "You're a lucky little girl," the nurse had said.

The wound healed. But the bullet left a scar in the shape of itself.

My mother, Newark, NJ, 1926

My mother would stroke it at night in the dark room where she and her sister slept. It was her emblem of bravery.

Her brother promised to teach her how to shoot hard and straight at bottles lined up on a bench in an alley near their house. Before their first lesson, Nathan took off for California. People with guns a lot bigger than his gun were after him he said.

My mother never held a gun again. But she would always remember the feel of the weapon and the sound it made when it went off. When her father shouted at her and teased her in a cold, mean way, and when her mother threw her clothes out the window because they were on the floor of her room, she imagined the gun in her pocket with her hand around it. In her daydreams, she would shoot up into the air and the sky would quiver.

Sixty years later on her deathbed, she kept at her feet a silver-tipped cane that looked like a rifle. The scar from the bullet wound was still on her thigh. She wagged a finger at me. "Get me to a hospital." I saw gun smoke in her eyes.

Sea Carousel

My father can't stop smiling when the sun comes out. He loves the wind and the sea and the sky. At age four I experience the magical power of motion as he lifts me high into the air and back down again. Up and down. Up and down. Each time I touch the sky, I grab for a fistful of clouds. My father places me on his shoulders, and I stretch my arms out wide. The morning sky is a powdery blue. The ocean yawns and sparkles. I watch the foam make scallops on the shore like giant cutout dolls.

It is low tide; my father takes my hand, and we wade into the water. As my legs disappear, I feel pebbles tickle my feet. He places a hand under my stomach, so I can kick in the bubbly blue water. I feel my body vibrate with the tug and rumble of the sea. I am a mermaid, a girl-fish, and a floating star. I shine and shimmer, splash, and swirl. "Keep it up," he says. "That's my girl." He takes my hands and gently twirls me around and around. I am on a carousel of sand, sea, and sky; I can see other mermaids as well as seahorses dancing on the horizon. I see a smudge of land that could be Russia, the country my father comes from.

The sun is pancake hot when we get out of the water and so is the sand. My father whisks me up under his arm and carries me up the steps to the lawn in front of our house. We dance on the squeaky grass next to the yellow tulips and the birdbath. He takes perfect little steps. I jump and stomp. We take an outdoor shower, letting the water tickle our skin.

Dad helps me change into shorts and a top, and we plop down on a chaise-lounge at the back of our low blue ranch house. A tree guards us from the sun. I curl up next to my father, who looks like a fuzzy bear with black hair on his chest. He smells of Coppertone and sweat. His round face has a ruddy color. His brown eyes are small and playful. He has wavy dark hair like mine.

"Dad," I say. "Tell me a story from when you were little. Did you have a pony? Did you have fun riding him?"

My father crinkles up his eyes, making them look even smaller. "No, I didn't have a pony. We didn't have fun in Russia, honey."

"Tell me something you did," I say. Dad's childhood is like a fish I want to catch.

My father sighs. His voice gets very quiet. His eyes aren't smiling and neither is his mouth. "I remember walking along a river on a cold night. I had a lantern in my hand, so I could see my way in the dark."

I wait for him to say something else, but he doesn't.

Boy with a Lantern

I imagine my father's family of origin: the house in Odessa; the river is ink blue under a sliver of moonlight. There is dust on the floor and shelves filled with jars of black cherries; the smell of herring singes the air. On the table there is a loaf of bread that is stale at the edges but still fresh at the center.

My father's father, Samuel, sits at the head of the table. His cheekbones are high; his face is impassive. He breaks the bread with long, tapered fingers. His wife Jenny sits at the opposite end of the table. She is wearing somber colors but has wild red hair and dreams of coming to America. My father sits to his mother's right; he is small and dark. His brown eyes are so soft in color they might melt. He is drinking borscht from a spoon one slurp at a time while his sister Sarah laughs. She is older than he is; she has spools of brown curls and a voice that sounds like an engine revving up. His brother Phil is very little. His face looks like a rubber stamp of itself. He looks at his father, who doesn't see him. "I'm hungry," he says. The bread defies his small teeth.

The mother stands up. Her tone is emphatic. "My sister, Esther

My father, circa 1911

has fresh bread. "Lou," she says to my father, who sits to attention and blinks his eyelashes. "Take the lantern. Walk by the river and get us some."

My father puts on a frayed blue jacket with brass buttons. He takes the lantern, which is almost as big as he is. He walks along the water holding the lantern tightly. The wind tastes of night. The distant moon looks almost blue against the dark sky. He is hungry for stars.

In the Middle of the Night

For Sylvia Wertheimer and Laura Wertheimer and the stars

When my cousin Lillian came to visit, she and I would pull down the shades in my room and turn out the lights. Then she would switch on her toy planetarium, and dots of light would appear on the ceiling. Lillian introduced me to Andromeda, the princess; Orion, the hunter; Cygnus, the swan; and Polaris, the North Star.

Lillian could bring alive these summer constellations any time of year.

The summer Lillian and her parents moved to California would be our last star show. She splashed the Big Dipper on the ceiling—seven bright stars: three forming the handle and four forming the bowl. She explained that long ago, when Africans were kept as slaves in the South, many escaped in the middle of the night by following the Big Dipper north to freedom.

After Lillian left, I learned to conjure up the stars when my mother's angry voice rang in my ears, or when my father's face looked like it might never smile again.

Lillian and I would grow up and fall in love with men who had roving eyes and loved themselves more than they did us. On the few occasions when I saw my cousin, she drank Scotch and spoke in a quiet, controlled voice. Neither of us mentioned the stars. We lost track of each other after a while.

A much later summer I went to the beach with a friend and her fifteen-year-old daughter. One night the daughter and another girl came running into the house to say that they'd been looking at the stars. I went outside to look with them. We stood under the sky, and they pointed to the Big Dipper—seven bright stars—and to Polaris in the north, which Lillian had said shone all year round. Feeling a familiar excitement, I walked toward them in the darkness.

Camp Picture

Big girls don't cry," my mother says. "Not even a whimper," she reminds me when she drops me off at sleepaway camp. It is my seventh summer. I wait for her letters. I know they will say, "I love you, and I will visit." Here in New Hampshire there are lots of trees and a lake that sparkles.

My mother arrives in a long full skirt and a white blouse. Her wavy brown hair almost touches her shoulders. I am wearing a white T-shirt and blue shorts and my curly brown hair is tied back in a ponytail. I walk toward her quietly in my small blue sneakers. The lawn is green and the sky is blue, and we look past each other as my father snaps our picture. I want to say, "Take me home. I hate it here even though the girls are nice, and I get to run wild with no one saying stop. I am no one's special little girl." My mother's long pale face and wide-green eyes with the faraway look tell me to keep these thoughts to myself. I bite into one of the cookies she has brought me. The soft chocolate melts in my mouth, and I say, "Yum," and my mother smiles.

In the picture taken of us that day my mother puts her arms

around me, while I look into the field beyond and then up at the sky. I don't remember her leaving or coming back. I know I am always waiting for her and pretending I am not. All things sweet will crystallize in the moment of her return.

Let's Fly

My mother is shouting; she sounds like a raging fire engine or maybe even louder. "Pick these things, up!" she commands my best friend Johnny C and me. Rubber tomahawks, jacks, balls and the pieces of my plastic tea set are tossed in every corner of my room.

Johnny C, who is wearing a brown cowboy print shirt, puts his hands on his hips and spins around to face her. He is Hopalong Cassidy after all, and nobody can tell him what to do. His cowlick stands straight up; no amount of Brylcreem can tame it. I like looking at the birthmark on his left cheek. "It's a free country," he says to my mother, who bursts into laughter watching him. Her anger has melted away; her eyes look gray and mischievous.

"Okay, kids, go outside; you can clean up later; enjoy the sunshine."

Johnny's sister Betsey is waiting in the living room. She is a college girl with a long brown ponytail pulled to one side. She has on red pedal pushers and a kind of half smile on her face that seems to say, "I'm pretty." She has a boyfriend called Snuckers, who isn't with her today. Once Johnny caught them kissing in the living room. Betsey is going to baby sit because my mother and father are driving into New York City. I wonder if my parents are going to talk during the long car ride over the George Washington Bridge; even at dinner, they seem to forget the other one is there. When I was little, I would sit between them in the front seat and the bridge would stretch like a giant's arm in front of us. Sometimes my mother would peel oranges, and we would pass the slices back and forth. I liked the warm line of our bodies and the chuckle in my father's throat.

Johnny, Betsey and I run out onto the lawn, which looks lime green in the sunshine, and then we run down the steep staircase to the beach. The sea is a little bit rough today; the waves are galloping toward us. The sand feels like sugar under my feet. Betsey strips down to her bathing suit and runs toward the shoreline; we follow her in our shorts, but she says, "Stop," in a tone that sounds so grown-up that we do as she tells us. Betsey dives under a wave and comes up and then dives under another.

Johnny tugs me by the arm and says, "I wanna show you something." He leads me all the way to the bluff, the place where the sand is almost a cliff and you can jump off. He has been daring me to come here with him ever since I came back from sleep-away camp, but when we get to the edge he stands behind me. "What if I break a leg and my mother makes me stay in bed and eat burned toast?"

I feel the wind on my face; I see fluffy white clouds above us; below us the sea is covered in diamonds. I take Johnny's hand, and suddenly we are flying against the sky. The sand is soft where we land, and we lie on our backs, letting the world spin around us.

"Are you alive?" Johnny asks.

"Yes," I say.

"I am too," he says.

I put my head on his shoulder to make sure we are both really okay.

"Quit it," he says but sort of hugs me.

After a while Johnny gets up. "Betsey might be looking for us," he says.

I imagine him watching the waves dance like ponies and the boats against the horizon that look like they were painted there with crayons. I just stay where I am, letting the sun dance on my legs and arms as if this moment were the only one there was or ever could be.

Chance Encounters

The summer I turn seven, storms roll across the New Jersey shore. Through our picture window, I can see waves charge like tigers. I can feel thunder rock the sky.

One night when it is raining hard, I get out of bed and walk into the living room. The blinds are wide open and my mother is standing in front of the window, looking into the distance. I hear my father shifting in their bed, pretending to sleep, making a funny low growl in his throat, which means, "Leave me alone."

My mother seems to come awake suddenly. As a streak of lightning fires the darkness, she puts her arm around me. "It's a dragon's tail," she says.

"It's a magic wand," I say. The sky becomes quieter.

"Go back to sleep," she says. She is watching the sea; she has forgotten me.

Another night I discover my father in the kitchen. In the dim light, I see he has a red summer blanket around his shoulders. Rain is drilling the roof and the windows; a sharp wind comes under the door. He heats some milk for me and pours it into my favorite cup with the picture of the White Rabbit on it. The milk tastes gentle and sweet. When I look up, I see tears on my father's cheeks.

In the last week of August, a storm gathers its breath and becomes a hurricane. As the sky rages, my mother, father and I run for cover into the small cozy den, which has no windows, and huddle together in a big upholstered chair, the color of earth. I sit on the cushion and my mother and father sit on the arms on either side of me; we all have our arms around each other; my father kisses my nose the way he did when I was very little. My mother's soft hand around mine feels like a velvet glove. "Everything is going to be all right," she says.

My father says, "We love you." When fall comes and the weather clears, my parents file for divorce.

PART II

The Boarding School Years

Boarding School Morning

This is my home away from home. The dining room is silent. The tables are ovals covered with starched white tablecloths. The silverware is harsh; the oatmeal is cool and lumpy. The girls around me are wearing blue jumpers and blouses with stiff white collars. I know my collar would scratch if I could feel it. I am learning not to breathe, not to move. The oatmeal trickles down my throat. I am seven. Everything is larger than I am.

The headmistress has a bun of braids and fiery gray eyes. A long bamboo stick sits next to her. She will hit us if we disobey. We are not allowed to speak at mealtime. I watch her survey the room for telltale signs of sound.

"Shush," the girl next to me says. I haven't spoken. I am forgetting the shape of words. I look around, but I have only partial vision. I see gray air and wallpaper covered with black and gray flowers. The headmistress rings a large silver bell. Plates and glasses clatter as girls who appear to be a lot bigger and older than I am clear the table.

The headmistress, Miss Simon, stands in front of the room, showing large white teeth. "Have a wonderful day, girls. A good breakfast starts the morning. Before we leave, let's welcome the new girls. Stand up and say hello," she urges a few other girls as well as me. Perhaps I only imagine that we stand in unison like actresses on a stage who have forgotten our lines or never knew them. I wonder if I am really there. I touch my hair, which has been tightly braided. I don't really try to smile. I am waiting for something to happen.

"For everything there is a season," I hear the headmistress say. "Fall is the season of new beginnings. Feel the leaves crunch under your feet. Give thanks for the blue sky." She laughs. "But don't let the wind get under your collars."

No one else laughs, but the girl next to me smiles: a little twist of her cheek. Then the dining room is infused with sound. Black chairs with spokes are being pushed into tables; feet are pounding on the hardwood floor. We pour down the stairs into the cloakroom. When the door swings open, fear and wonder churn in my stomach. I see a towering sky and the silhouette of a hill. I follow the other girls down a narrow path and under a grape arbor. The path becomes wider; thick trees stand on either side of us. I see the schoolhouse in the distance, brown and white like a gingerbread castle.

I walk toward it, taking careful steps in my new brown oxfords. I put one foot in front of the other. I do it again.

Making Music

I learned to play the piano by rote. Dutifully I pounded on the keys as if they might break under my fingers. At ten, without my mother's permission, I signed up for piano lessons at my boarding school. She agreed once she saw my enthusiasm. The piano teacher always wore the same blue-flowered dress and smelled of dried flowers and determination. I don't remember her name. Miss Luppine or Miss Lupline, I think. She was thick at the waist and moved without sound. Haltingly I learned to read music. I was intrigued with the notes, the way they might fly off the page and sing. I liked the sound of the clanking keys. What I really wanted to make was magic: the twilight sway of Chopin. I wanted the keys to shout out melody. My notes could float where I could not go—high into the clouds like a harp connected to the stars. The fact that I had no talent didn't deter me. If my playing sounded leaden, I could make ethereal music that only my inner ear could hear.

At night when the other girls were studying European history, I descended to the room beneath the study hall where a grand piano the color of honey was waiting for me. I stood up letting my fingers fly soundlessly above the keys, tossing my head back, making way for flourishing music.

Waking Up

It is 1960, and I am certain John F. Kennedy will win the upcoming presidential election. In televised debates against Nixon, Kennedy knows when to smile, his hair is just right, and his eyes are quick and intelligent. He says we have a voice in how our country works and can make it better.

Nobody else at boarding school recognizes Kennedy as the hero he is. One weekend, my mother and stepfather take me to a Kennedy rally, where I get a picture postcard of Kennedy that I keep under my pillow so that I can talk to him and give him encouragement. The headmistress tells me that a young Catholic can never become president. I disagree. Miracles can happen. The other girls laugh at me and say I have a crush on him.

On election night I lie awake and listen to the other girls snore. I never close my eyes. "You can do it, John," I say into the darkness. Kennedy wants Mexicans, Puerto Ricans, and Negroes to be treated equally under the law. When he gets elected, I'm going to ask him if he'll give Manhattan back to the Indians. I keep my radio close to my ear. At three a.m. Kennedy is projected to be the winner. I did it. I can't contain my excitement. I jump down onto the cold floor and wake up every single girl with the news.

Making Out

The room is dark and cold. We pull the blankets close in our bunk beds. Makiko is on the top bunk opposite mine. I like her slanted eyes. Her mother left the family when she was five to become a singer in California. I've seen her mother's picture. Dark hair like a waterfall. Eyes like thin almonds and the hint of a smile.

Lots of men wanted to kiss her mother Makiko says. He was taller than Makiko's father and twice as charming, the man her mother ran off with. Makiko had lived in foster homes before she came to boarding school. She made out with boys on beds, floors, in closets even in an alley in the Bronx. Like me, Makiko is twelve. Her boyfriend Peter is twenty. He thinks she's sixteen because she has a voice like slow jazz, and she walks swinging her arms outward like she's making her own space in the world.

"It's like this," Makiko says. "Peter puts his tongue in my mouth."

Slimy, I think. "And then what?" I ask.

"Our tongues touch and slide around," Makiko says.

I imagine a tongue dance. Two snails slithering out of their shells.

"Ugh," I say. "What next?"

Makiko sighs. "We do it again. Our tongues I mean." She talks real deep in her throat like she's done this a lot.

I'm not that interested in tongues: their rhythms and synchronicities and secret probings into the cavern of the mouth to seek and explore. I like the fact that the subject is forbidden. Here in this New Jersey haven of roses and thorns, where our parents have dropped us off to figure life out for ourselves, Makiko is my pipeline to the outside world.

Marlboro Country

My friend Barb and I help the headmistress, Miss Simon, fold clothes in the attic while she tells us about her Minnesota childhood. We listen to her talk about the thick white snow and the cold blue sky and how she spun down a hill on a toboggan, and then as a reward she takes us down to the kitchen and gives us cookies and milk and a plump kiss on each of our cheeks. "You're such good girls," she says.

Outside on the playground Barb kicks a stick. "I don't want to be good," she mutters.

"Neither do I," I say. I don't sound as certain as she does, but I'd like to.

That night while my fifth grade teacher, Miss Charles, is officiating at study hall, Barb steers me down the stairs to Miss Charles's room, where a half-empty pack of Marlboros is sitting on the rolltop desk. Barb filches two and puts them in her pocket as I hold my breath. She keeps them in a shoebox at the bottom of the closet until we hatch a plan.

One chilly October morning before the other girls get up, we steal out of the house, the cigarettes safe in the pocket of Barb's red parka. We run fast and hard across the grass, stopping between two pine trees next to a shrub; the blue gray sky looks askance at us. Barb lights one match and then another. The wind won't cooperate. Finally, we see fire. She hands me a cigarette. I put the tip in my mouth and pull hard.

"Are you smoking?" she asks.

I nod forcefully.

"You're not," she says. "I don't see any smoke."

I take the cigarette away from my mouth. "I might be," I say.

I feel grown up and evil.

She lights the other cigarette with what seems like magical speed and takes a puff. She coughs so loud I see a bird's nest quiver.

When she comes up for air, she assures me, "The Marlboro man on TV coughs too."

I don't question her authority. We grind out the guilty butts and run across the dewy grass.

We never tell anybody what we did but at night after study hall when a man on horseback seems to gallop through the TV set with a Marlboro between his teeth, we look at each other and smile.

Good Friends

Barb's thick blond hair stood up in tufts in contrast to my smooth dark waves. She didn't believe in Santa Claus or the tooth fairy or teachers who were always right and knew everything, while I flirted with all these possibilities.

I was seven and she was eight when we met. Squirreling her way up to the top of a giant pine, she would leave me awestruck and dizzy on the ground. "Come on up," she would shout.

I could hear my heart beating. "Next time," I promised. But I didn't keep my word.

Barb would ride her red two-wheeler bike down a wide green hill that curved around a tree, posting to gain speed and then putting her feet on the handlebars, letting the wind carry her, as I pedaled behind her on my blue bike, going faster and faster almost sure I could fly.

At night, sleeping in narrow beds that were lined up in rows, Barb and I would tie bathrobe cords together and cast them across the girl in the bed between us, connecting us in the dark.

"Night," Barb would whisper. "Don't let the bedbugs bite."

Barbara and me, circa 1962

"Night," I would say.

Then we would both pull on the cord to make sure the other one was there. We nursed each other through the chicken pox, the mumps and our parents' divorces before we were ten. We hid under the same dark wood desk with the crooked legs during safety drills in response to the threat of Khrushchev's bomb.

At twelve, when I became intrigued with a new girl named Ariana, who came from Colombia, South America, and spoke and wrote in Spanish, making elegant backward questions marks, Barb regarded me with disdain and dedicated herself to her stamp collection and exploring the marsh beyond the school for frogs and wild turtles. If she had a sad look on her face when I saw her at mealtime or curled up reading a mystery novel in her bed at night, I made sure not to pay close attention.

Because our parents were friends and because we liked each other more than we let on, we would spend time together on holidays. One Christmas when I was eleven and Barb was twelve, my mother suggested that we watch a play called *Waiting for Godot* on television. Two clownish-looking men kicked around the meaning of life in words I only half understood.

"When do you think Godot is coming?" I asked Barb. "I want to get some cookies."

"Never," she smirked. "That's the whole point of the play."

We both knew the meaning of never. Our parents were divorced and were never going to live together again. We could never see them except for every two weeks on visiting Sunday.

"I'm going to wait anyway," I said. "He might show up."

Despite her cynicism, Barb waited too.

We went to different high schools and colleges, visiting each other from time to time. I studied literature in New York, while she moved out West and bought a horse, and then married and had two kids; in the years that followed, she built a successful business as a stamp dealer, while I tried my hand at writing and teaching. My relationships with men were intense and fleeting. Barb's husband, Bill, who wore cowboy boots and had a lisp, could finesse the guitar and other women with equal agility; she forgave him his indiscretions for the sake of keeping the family together. Fifteen years into their union, he took off for the Colorado hills with his secretary, leaving her crying herself to sleep from rage as much as from sadness.

Some years later, we would travel the rocky coast of Spain, stopping to swim in the Mediterranean near a ruined castle. I remember the fat orange moon that hung over our rented Barcelona apartment building and the sky thick with perfumed smog. Decades would pass; we would lose our parents, our youth; Barb would become a grandmother of five, and we'd both garner a bit of wisdom. And yet that night, as if there were no other, we stood shoulder to shoulder on a terrace of smooth stone, watching the moon like a giant coin in the sky move toward us.

Graham Crackers and Pears

The floor pillows are puffy clouds on a light gray carpet. Two day beds are covered with gold brocade fabric to look like couches. There is a glass cocktail table shaped like a giant square with a swan on an ivory panel peering through the glass.

My mother and I sit on low black stools in front of the table, munching on the grilled cheese sandwiches she has made for us on a small elaborate grill in the tiny room that passes for a kitchen. The windows behind us show a light gray sky; the interior light in the room is soft yet bright. My mother brings me chocolate milk and graham crackers for dessert. I can tell by the way she walks that she is happy; she is moving through a world of beauty, sweet tastes, and soft sounds.

She is not angry today. Her eyes are pure green with no flecks of blue and gray. Her newly dyed blond hair makes a halo around her head. She laughs lightly without the gravel I usually hear in her voice; she touches my cheek with offhand affection. Since her separation from my father, she has acquired two boyfriends, one of whom will die suddenly, the other whom she will marry and glory in and regret the decision. On my vacation from boarding school, she welcomes me into the first and only home where I will feel her joy, her youth, and her belief that a little can go a long way.

She brings cold golden pears to the cocktail table, cuts them in slices, puts a slice in her mouth, and savors its sweetness. I bite on a slice too.

I hear the ticking of a clock that shows you its inner workings as part of its design. There is a scent of fall in the air. I don't want to break the stillness by darting into the kitchen. When I come back this mother may be gone. She will have sharp nails and eyes the color of a rained-on sky.

Mona Lisa Giacondo

It is visiting Sunday. I am thirteen and my father is taking me to New York City to view Leonardo Da Vinci's *Mona Lisa* at the Metropolitan Museum. He arrives wearing earmuffs, a snug black hat, and a bulky black coat. He moves heavily in his gray snow boots. I walk next to him in my squeaky red boots and heavy-red corduroy coat with the fake fur collar, feeling the chill of his sadness. "You're a half–orphan now," he says as we trudge down the driveway toward his car. Does this mean that each parent loves me half as much since his or her divorce?

The country roads are bleak and slippery as my father steers onto the Palisades Parkway where snow-covered rocks stand on either side of us like small mountains. I feel the car is a cave and my father's voice the only earthly sound. "Mona Lisa Giacondo," he says with a pronounced growl. "Repeat after me."

I try but the "Giacondo" doesn't rise to his standard of linguistic perfection. I hear a disgruntled clicking in his throat as the car rocks on a mound of ice before finding level ground again.

An hour later we ascend the icy steps of the Metropolitan only

Me in a thoughtful mood, 1963

to wait on a long line outside a dim room where the masterpiece is on display. As I shuffle back and forth, I see the angry twist of my father's lips. "Who do you think you are, Princess Margaret? You're going to wait like every other ordinary person."

My father, my mother says, is jealous of her new boyfriends. He thinks they are swashbuckling Casanovas with pockets full of cash, and he doesn't want me to enter a degenerate life of privilege along with her. My father tells me that the woman in the painting may have been the wife of a wealthy landowner, but her true identity is shrouded in mystery.

Finally we enter the gallery where the Mona Lisa rests against a red curtain. There is a strange light giving definition to her white cheeks. Her eyes are dark and playful; her mouth is curved in what might be a smile. "Mona Lisa Giacondo," my father whispers, and I know I am expected to mimic his inflection. I stay silent, adopting the insolent curve of her cheeks.

My father takes hold of my arm and pulls me to the left, so the man next to us can get a better view. I want to shout at him, "Let go of me." But instead I pull away, running into the entranceway of the museum with the high echoing ceilings and then up another stone staircase that is wide and imposing, finally tripping over my own foot and scraping the face of my knee to a bloody pulp. I try to keep the Mona Lisa Giacondo smile on my face but pain rears up and turns it into a grimace as my father bends down over me to see what has happened. For the first time in months his own face softens around the mouth. "It hurts. Doesn't it?" he says.

Magic Tricks

I am eight going on nine the first time I hear his footsteps on the gravel driveway of my boarding school. He isn't my stepfather then, just my mother's funny, fat friend. He has a firecracker smile and a cap slung over one eye. He does a little soft-shoe shuffle like Fred Astaire in the movie, *Top Hat* that I once watched on my mother's black and white TV in her New York City apartment. Outside I tried it myself. Side step. Side step. I liked the slide of the city sidewalk smooth under my feet.

My boarding school is all country. It is spring. Giant pines stand in their green dresses; a grape arbor runs a wreath across the sky. I can see him squinting in his green silk jacket and white golf cap; he hooks an arm through my mother's as if she is his perfect sweetheart. Her new white blond hair glows next to his shoulder; her perfume smells like honey; he leans closer to her. She has a green-eyed, faraway look as if the clouds were speaking to her.

We go to a restaurant on top of a hill that slants into the sky. Through a picture window, we can see grass and sky and red and yellow tulips that stand up in rows. Inside our tablecloth is perfectly white and pressed. Tiny wild flowers in a smoky blue vase are on the table. We sit up straight with party table manners. My mother sits to his right and I to his left. When he takes off his cap, I see that his head is bald like the back of a skinned rabbit. I wonder if the wind and the rain will hurt it, but I don't ask him. Careful not to spill on my blue Sunday jumper and white blouse, I take little bites of my hamburger. The crusty bun melts in my mouth. A bee whizzes back and forth in front of our window. We may be speaking, but I can't hear us. My mind goes away and then comes back again.

My mother pushes her plate away first. She is wearing a silk cream-colored dress. Flowers with green stems and blue petals are embroidered on the front. She has a matching scarf that she keeps tossing over her shoulder. As she blows smoke rings like the caterpillar in *Alice's Adventures in Wonderland*, I like the way the smoke twirls and disappears. Its one way I know my mother is real. Another is when she is talking, tossing out big words and small ones. She says, "Richard, why don't you show us a magic trick?"

When the chocolate ice cream comes, Richard pretends to pull a quarter out of his ear and then presses it into my palm. The quarter is cold; his hand is warm and solid around mine.

"Watch this," he says, dropping a sugar cube into a glass of water; we see the cube fall to the bottom. When he fishes it out with a spoon, it has his initials on it: RWH. "Richard Walter Harmon," he says, kind of gruff and shy. "I'll show you how it's done," he promises. "Next time."

I know my mother is leaning toward me because her perfume

moves with her. I check her eyes for storm clouds, but there aren't any. She isn't wearing her painted smile but a real one. I almost feel like smiling too. A patch of cold comes from Richard's direction. His lips appear thin and tight. Somewhere deep inside I shiver.

My mother is speaking. "Richard studied magic in London with a famous magician," she says. "He knows hundreds of tricks."

I know my mother can embroider the truth to make a story more interesting. Richard smiles and winks at me, kind of pretend evil like Captain Hook just before he sends the pirates after Peter. Sunshine comes through the windows and paints us all in afternoon colors.

Second Wedding

I was ten when my mother and stepfather decided one day to get married, enlisting a court clerk as witness. I imagine them walking up the courthouse steps in Brooklyn Heights.

My mother is wearing a Cheshire-cat smile; her blond hair is puffed and sprayed. Her shoulders are thrust back; her chin leads the way.

Arm-and-arm they walk into the judge's chambers. My stepfather is dressed all in black except for the blood-red tie against his white shirt and his huge victory smile. At sixty-five, he is marrying a woman of thirty-nine, which fills him with equestrian pride. His heart skips a beat; he fumbles for a nitroglycerin in his pocket. The yellow pill melts under his tongue as if it had never been. My mother folds her hand in his; she likes the velvety texture of his skin.

The judge asks them to profess unending devotion for each other; they say their 'I dos' and trot down the stairs into the open air. A spring wind propels them forward. The sky, a gray cape over their heads, decides to rain on them. "Come on," my stepfather says, taking off his jacket and throwing it over my mother's beige silk suit. He watches her high heels make patterns in the street.

"Forever and always," echo through her mind. What will they say to each other all the rest of their lives? How will they breathe the same air? How much charm can she energize him with? How long can she tantalize him with her beauty? How can she keep her secret self alive in the cramped space of a marriage? The rain stops and she smells the green of spring in Brooklyn Heights. She knows she is lovelier than any tree or building.

He links his arm through hers and feels his younger self enter his body. There is peace and tenderness in the way he steers her around the corner. He wants to keep walking, feeling the air and the soft shimmer of her flesh. What if this moment could become their lives, rarefied and calm?

What does it Mean to be Jewish?

It doesn't mean anything to me to be Jewish," I told my fifth grade teacher, Miss Charles. Since I was the only Jewish girl in a Presbyterian boarding school, she was determined to make me aware of my heritage.

Miss Charles, a woman from a large Catholic family, had a sister, Maria, who had married a Jewish man named Ben, who had a fuzzy beard and intense blue eyes and knew a reservoir of stories about the bible that Miss Charles in turn told me. But tales of nomadic Jews crossing the desert in blistering heat to escape the Egyptians gave me no ancestral quiver. My parents had cast off what they saw as the shackles of their Orthodox Jewish childhoods; they preferred Christmas to Chanukah, and so did I.

When the bible didn't stir me, Miss Charles appealed to my intellect. She informed me that I was part of an illustrious line of great thinkers: She explained that Freud, who had discovered the key to the unconscious mind, and Einstein, who had solved the riddle of the universe, had both been Jewish. I felt no point of identification with either of these geniuses.

Attending Presbyterian Church on Sundays with my classmates, I was mesmerized by the minister's soft voice, large Adam's apple, and sweet smile. I enjoyed watching the big-bosomed women in the choir in their long red robes heave and sigh as they sang hymns, and I loved singing along with them. The Amens were my favorite—the way we let them build in our chests and swell into resounding song. During one of his sermons, the minister reminded us to respect our Jewish neighbors and friends. I never owned up to being one of them.

I remember the first time Miss Charles told us about the Nazi regime in Europe. It was late November and the sky was almost dark outside our window. She took out a matchbook and struck fire; blowing the match out, she explained that Jews had been extinguished in gas chambers, and their remains burned in ovens, the air of the death camps carrying the scent of their flesh.

When Adolf Eichmann went on trial in Israel for ordering many of these killings, Miss Charles invited me to her room and turned on the black and white TV. Eichmann, a man with a pencil-thin mouth, large ears, and a refined nose, stood in a glass cage before his accusers. As witnesses recounted his crimes, pictures came on the screen of skeletal bodies, some of them still alive, being dumped into a wide chasm in the earth.

"Being Jewish may not mean anything to you," Miss Charles said, "but it would have meant something to Hitler. If you had lived in Europe during the Second World War, you might have been one of those corpses."

I felt a shivering deep inside me both from fear and excitement. I had a legacy and that made me and other Jewish people part of history. Still a part of me was angry at Miss Charles for handing it to me since fitting in seemed more important than being singled out as special. But when she invited me to a Chanukah party at her sister's house, I accepted out of curiosity and enjoyed playing spin the dreidel with a girl named Susan, who had curly red hair and a twinkle in her eyes. Susan lit a Chanukah candle and handed it to me to place in a silver menorah, so we could mark the eighth day of Chanukah. Watching the candles glow in the cheerful room, I wondered if the story Miss Charles had told me about an ancient oil lamp with only enough oil for a day really burned for eight to commemorate the rebirth of Judaism after the Macabees, a few brothers who gave their name to an army and drove the Syrians from the temple in Israel.

Over Christmas vacation my mother and stepfather and I flew down to Florida and so did my friend Gena and her mother, Mrs. Harris, who invited me to a beach club where waiters in starched white jackets served hamburgers on crispy buns. The sun made the water in the kidney shaped pool glitter. After Gena and I swam back and forth and wrapped ourselves in big white towels, she said, "Did you know there used to be a sign out front that said, 'No Jews and Dogs Allowed.' Even though the sign isn't there anymore, it's still true my mother says." Gena knitted her brow and looked at me quizzically. "What are you going to say if someone asks you if you're Jewish?"

I felt the sting of her accusation. "I don't know," I said.

For the rest of the afternoon, my breath felt tight in my chest. Should I wait to be discovered? Should I call my mother and ask her to pick me up? Gripping the sides of the chaise lounge, I watched the palm trees sway in the December wind.

A few hours later when we were leaving, a friendly waiter turned to us and said, "Merry Christmas girls."

I could feel my heart beating. I took a deep breath. "Happy Chanukah," I said. "I'm Jewish."

That night Gena's mother called to apologize to my mother for what Gena had said. I kept thinking about the sign painted in large black letters.

After the holidays, Miss Charles gave me a thin paperback book about a concentration camp called Bergen-Belsen. In it I saw pictures of Jewish prisoners dressed in striped work overalls; their cheeks were sunken; their eyes were huge and sorrowful; some of them were children. After I had studied the book from cover to cover, I showed it to the other girls. Some of them said, "Gross." And others stared in horror and amazement. I felt a kinship with the people in the pictures.

The Diary of Anne Frank was my favorite of all the books Miss Charles introduced to me. Pretending to travel back in time, I would visit Anne in her Secret Annex, and there on her narrow bed, we would speak in hushed whispers about a world gone mad with hate, and would tell each other how fervently we believed that no matter what some people did or said mankind was essentially good. In my version of her story, Anne did not die in Bergen-Belsen; she remained undiscovered and when the war ended we walked arm-and-arm down an Amsterdam street in the brazen sunlight, two proud Jewish girls, happy to be alive.

The Last Time

After study hall at boarding school, we would line up our chairs in front of a small black and white TV set and watch the crime drama, *Perry Mason*. I sat in a seat behind a girl named Vicki Reyes. I was twelve and Vicki was eleven. She had light brown hair that fell over her shoulders. She never turned around because she, like the rest of us, was intent on watching the story unfold.

When Perry Mason winked at the audience in the opening scene, we would let out little yelps of pleasure. He had brooding dark eyes, full lips and a wide nose with flared nostrils. His dark suit and the fine-white handkerchief in his breast pocket remained unruffled even as the plot thickened. As a criminal attorney, Perry Mason was confronted with blackmail, double identities, subterfuge, and murder. He drove around in his black convertible, stopping in cheerful coffee shops for apple pie and coffee in between dangerous interrogations. Vicki bit on her nails when we thought a man was about to lunge at Perry with an ice pick, and I averted my eyes. We giggled and touched hands for luck, knowing Perry could get out of any jam and everything would work out perfectly.

In the courtroom, women with throaty voices in mink stoles and white gloves up to their elbows confessed when faced with Perry's inquisitive scowl, his incredulous eyebrows, and target-perfect evidence. The men, who chain-smoked and said they knew the score, also admitted what they had done. Perry's falsely accused clients always went free. The music would climb like a wolf's ascending howl as Perry got closer to forcing someone to shout, "I did it."

Murder rarely took place on screen, but one night an embezzler shot a gambler with a pistol. Vicki whispered, "My mother shot a man when she was drunk, but she missed."

Vicki had told me that her mother hid vodka bottles in dresser drawers and under the sink and that she would stagger and slur her words, and I had promised Vicki that her mother would stop drinking if she asked her to very sweetly. I told her not to worry, but she said, "I have to."

Vicki and I both went home for summer vacation, Vicki to the Bronx, where her mother lived with a man named Kit, and I to my mother and stepfather's apartment in Brooklyn. One Sunday when my mother brought home the *Daily News,* Vicki's picture was on the cover. Her tangled brown hair and pleading brown eyes spoke to the reader, "Help me," they said. The story explained that help would have been too late. A random intruder had murdered Vicki while her mother and Kit were out on a drunken binge. There was a picture of her mother in a long beige dress looking grief-stricken and forlorn. No real-life Perry Mason was there to unravel the case, and as far as I know the murderer was never caught. Vicki's black and white image on the tabloid cover was the last time I saw her.

Getting Ready

It is October 1962. My eighth grade classmates and I, who are scheduled to graduate in the spring, are sitting at small wooden desks carved with graffiti while our teacher, Miss Elfman, tells us in methodical detail about the power struggle between Soviet Premier Khrushchev and President John F. Kennedy. Kennedy has set up a naval blockade against Soviet ships that are headed for Cuba with a cargo of missiles. If the Soviets don't retreat, the U.S. has promised to attack. We may be on the brink of nuclear war.

Later, in the dorm room I share with six other girls, I look at my reflection in the full-length mirror. My baby fat has receded into curves; my small features are almost beautiful. I am not ready to be erased from the planet.

Mary Beth, who sleeps in the bed next to mine, has a plan. If we don't want to die virgins, she tells me and another roommate, we should dress in tight jeans and sweaters, tease and spray our hair, and climb out the window with her once the other girls are asleep. She is going to meet Pete, the boy with sleek black hair who works at the gas station down the road. He may have friends for us.

It is cold when we sneak out. We land on a stone path and run across a wide field to the dirt road. But the gas station is closed, and Pete is nowhere in sight. Above us the moon is bright and almost full. We race back across the grass, laughing, and finally fall to the ground and lie on our backs, out of breath. My mind is free of fears and plans about the future. I feel the warmth of the girls on either side of me and see the broad expanse of starry sky above.

PART III

High School and Beyond

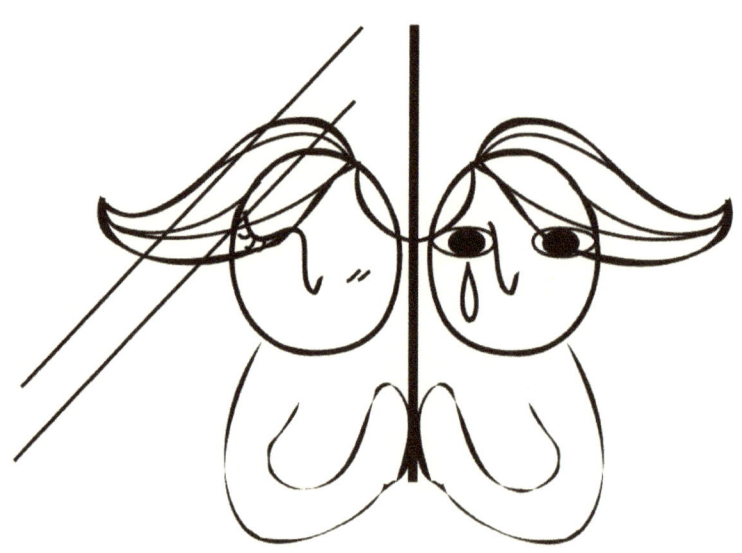

I Wasn't Invited

I walk on asphalt instead of grass. Buildings that loom like monsters come out of the pavement. There are streets named Pineapple, Joralemon, Henry, and Hicks and very few trees. My high school is a stone building covered in ivy. Inside there is a chapel with stained glass windows, muting and diffusing the light. There are classrooms with wooden floors and desks and teachers who astonish me with their slant on life: Mrs. Stepel is convinced that God is a phantom, Mrs. Langford discusses the matrix of DNA and the neutrons and electrons that seize the air. My English teacher, Miss Fitch, has us read *My Antonia* in which the frigid Nebraska winter is as cold as I feel in this alien world of girls who talk up in class and carry leather pocketbooks. After school I walk by the river where the Statue of Liberty is small yet tangible in the distance, a green lady I could pick up like a chess pawn and carry to victory like my father in an intense game of chess with his brother. In this urban landscape, I feel uninvited. Where is the girl who could do cartwheels on a wide field? Where are the headmistress, the teachers and the stone schoolhouse that was home for seven years?

I can't wait for gym class, so I can fling my body over a leather horse and pretend it is a real one I could ride through the rickety wooden doors of the building and ascend into the sky. A girl named Kara has a locker next to mine. I like her easy smile and the way one bucktooth bends over another. She wears a cape instead of a coat and her blue eyes seem to have different depths. She loves the way the subway grumbles and stops and lets you off almost anywhere you want to go. Greenwich Village is her territory; she lives with her mother and her brother and her sister in a townhouse on Perry Street. Her parents are divorced, like mine. In the late fall and winter afternoons we walk on cobblestone streets lit by old-fashioned lanterns. We peer into windows, where pink light casts an eerie gleam on other people's sofas and chairs. Sometimes her brother Brian joins us; I can't tell if his gray eyes are cruel or kind.

Our gym teacher, Mrs. Lauther, who has a matter-of-fact voice and always wears boring blue shorts, announces that six girls can become cheerleaders for a neighboring boy school's football team in the spring. Kara and I know our handstands and back flips are impeccable and should gain us entry into the world of pompoms, high white socks, short blue skirts and tight sweaters. But when Mrs. Lauther surveys us at tryouts, her mouth curls disdainfully. We are passed over for girls who move with studied eloquence and less energy.

My mother, who believes whatever I do is a reflection on her, is furious when she hears the news. How dare they turn a blind eye to my acrobatic talent, and my newly acquired ability to twirl a baton? Dressed in an elegant suit made of upholstery fabric, one of her own designs, she marches into the principal's office, despite my wild insistence for her to mind her own business, and with her astonishing talent for persuasion, secures me a position on the team.

The cheerleading outfit scratches when I put it on, and I decide that I don't want to be part of the dancing and tumbling without Kara. "Not even a thank you," my mother shouts. Her nostrils quiver with rage, but I don't care.

At night when my mother and stepfather are sleeping, I spring into a handstand, letting my legs touch the closet door, making a bow of my body.

When John Kennedy takes a bullet through his head on national television, Kara and I and her brother Brian watch the replay on her RCA television set. Each time I see Jacqueline Kennedy crawl out of the car in fear, each time I see John Kennedy slump like a mannequin into the upholstered seat, I imagine it won't happen the next time. Kara says with wisdom and optimism I don't feel, "He isn't really dead. He'll always be a part of history."

Winter covers the streets with snow and Brooklyn Heights looks white and new. As Kara and I walk down Grace Court Alley toward the river, the Statue of Liberty salutes us and we wave back at her; Kara's red scarf stands out against the cold, blue sky. When Kara comes to my house for lunch one Saturday, my mother and stepfather are enchanted with her easy smile and tranquil manner. My mother forgets to be angry and makes cranberry muffins, and I get permission to visit Kara's house whenever I want to.

Sometimes her brother Brian joins us on our walks through Greenwich Village. He is sixteen and his voice sounds deep and musical. We stop in front of a pink townhouse where a woman in a gray sweater is standing in the window of her kitchen washing dishes; her hands move with such precision that they seem to have fallen into a dance.

"She's a sculptor," Brian says. "She makes miniature statues out of stone." He takes my hand, showing me that one could fold into my palm. Rain begins to fall, darkening the sky at first lightly and then with a hard insistent rhythm. We take cover under our parkas and race past the streetlamps into the foyer of the narrow townhouse where Kara and Brian and her mother and sister live. As Kara races up the stairs to feed the five cats, Brian, who smells faintly of mint leaves, brushes his lips against mine.

Kara and I follow an early spring wind into Central Park past the duck pond; we climb high, moss-covered rocks that carry us into the sky. The clouds are moving quickly, and buildings of brick, glass and steel make a circle around us, welcoming us into the city.

Table Talk

We sit around a mahogany table covered with a starched white cloth. My mother and stepfather sit opposite one another, and I sit between them. The plates are white and round, silent as moons and as cold. What are we eating? Is there a world beyond this room?

My mother arches her back. Her streaked blond hair is as still as the air. Her words come in clicks and jolts. Sometimes she shrieks like a stereo that has gone out of tune. She is describing her shopping expedition to New York City, her shuffling through sales racks and bins in search of cashmere sweaters and silk dresses for phenomenally low prices. When she discovers a subtle rip or tear, she convinces the cashier to mark the item down further. Like a seasoned cabbie, she navigates the maze of Manhattan streets, going from store to store, and then at dusk she drives fast and easy across the Brooklyn Bridge, leaving the glitter of the skyline behind her, a stylish desperado returning home. I watch her as she speaks, the fumes and secretions of her mouth, and her haughty smile pulled tight at the corners.

My stepfather sits opposite her, eating spaghetti out of a bowl.

He is wearing a blue nightshirt; he is ailing. I hear the clicking of his fork, and the slurp of the noodles. The tomato sauce attaches itself to his lips, and he licks it away.

What am I doing? I am watching and waiting for the medieval horse and its mammoth rider to gallop out of the painting behind my stepfather, so I can climb into the saddle and travel with them. This is one of my mother's many artistic purchases from a thrift shop on Third Avenue. The sheer dimension of the painting rivets the viewer's attention. The horse is of a palomino color, proud and gallant; the rider is wearing a steel helmet and matching breastplates. I feel my mother studying the painting along with me, bending her long thin face in submission to its power. She envisions herself riding the horse bareback along a pristine beach; her hair, which is once again long and dark and lustrous, catches the sunlight. She watches the place where the sky and the sea meet.

My stepfather's thoughts lift him out of his tired body. He has become a young alderman on a street corner, raising the aspirations of his immigrant constituency: the Jews of Brownsville with their pushcarts and dreams. Hard work and determination will call forth manna from the sky he promises them. Their collective breath lingers in the cool March air around him, fanning him with gratitude. The shock of reentering the present moment causes him to shout. "Gertrude," he says to my mother, "get me some water!"

As my mother stands up, he turns to me. "Sit up straight. Don't call your mother 'she'."

Have I spoken?

Shopping

My mother is shouting. "Get over here," she says. The air is charged with her energy. We are in Alexander's department store in downtown Brooklyn, where she tears through the racks, holding up dresses: One is made of black velvet while the other, ribbed in green felt, is shaped like a Christmas tree. "Look at the quality of the fabric," she sighs, running her hand over the thick cotton as if it might respond to her touch.

"This one," my mother decides, taking the green dress into the fitting room.

At fifteen I have begun to put on weight. Suddenly I wish my body were a lump of clay I could sculpt into a firmer, leaner version of itself. My mother throws the dress at me and then impatiently walks over and yanks it over my head. She pulls it down over my hips, but it clings stubbornly to my waist. I think I am crying, but the tears are internal. Finally my mother tugs hard enough for the dress to descend and flair outward. I look at my reflection and see a pattern of red and green lines as if I've been painted in stripes. My mother is watching me, but her gaze is not intense. It seems to be

My mother and me, 1964

shifting to another time and place. "I had a dress like that when I was your age," she says. She touches my cheek with a warm knuckle. "You look pretty, honey. Really."

Sailing

The boat is on its side perpendicular to the sky. I touch the rudder and the world spins around me. The bay is remarkably blue and the sky is so close I imagine touching its tender skin.

This is a place beyond fear where the wind is gentle and insistent in my ears and the rush of water invites me to listen. Where am I going? I have no sense of the boat moving forward, only the circular swaying and rocking and spinning motion.

It is the tilt I love best, the way the sailboat stands on its side, and I can see the sail, fluttering with a sound smaller than the wind.

I am lean and tan in my sixteenth summer. I have on white shorts and my dark hair is cropped close to my head. At sailing camp, I have learned to make knots, rig a sail, and drop an anchor. Today, I take the rudder for the first time and let the rush and fall of the wind carry me. I am sure of everything—that the sky won't fall, that the boat won't capsize, that the chain of sadness behind and before me will evaporate into foam. There is only the hum of the wind and the murmur of water with me on it, only these things.

Sewing

The sun was beginning to dance along the wide Harlem street when my mother and I drew up in a taxicab to Alice Williams's apartment. It was ten in the morning on a Saturday in June as we climbed the four flights of stairs to her door. She swung it open and smiled at us, showing dashing white teeth against her dark skin.

"You girls sound like a herd of elephants," she said. She was wearing a brightly colored smock. Her hair was made up of tight gray curls. She was tall and a little thick around the middle. Her eyes were soft and brown and had a special light in them. She held her head high and walked toward us in a way that was at once solemn and playful. "Sit down and have some cookies," Alice said.

My mother made herself comfortable in an oak rocking chair, while I chose a wooden bench that was low to the ground. Sunlight came in the window, making the pink and white walls look like springtime. Originally from St. Thomas, Alice said she wanted the color of the tropics to be with her always. There was a picture on the wall of her husband George, who had a long thin face and quizzical eyebrows; he had died suddenly of a heart attack at the dinner table, leaving Alice and their three young daughters to fend for themselves. Alice liked to imitate George's laugh, the way it sounded like a horse's neigh and made her laugh too. In another picture, her granddaughter, Louisa, who was wearing a long black V-neck dress, appeared tall and regal, like her grandmother. She lived in Chicago and was studying to be an opera singer. Alice promised that one day soon we would meet her when she came to visit.

Alice was a dressmaker with a deft hand and a sewing machine that hummed with industry as she tapped its pedal with her long tapered foot. She had been working as a seamstress in a Manhattan thrift shop when she met my mother, a regular customer. My mother liked to say that they had become conspirators in creating beauty. She would provide Alice with the fabric and ideas for her designs, and Alice would bring them to life. Together they made a strapless dress in black brocade, a brightly colored sequined jacket trimmed in fur, a fitted white satin gown that made my mother look like an exquisite mermaid. Aunt Aida, my mother's sister, whistled when she saw her. She said, "Your mother is a hard act to follow, isn't she?"

Today Alice was altering a dress for me; one I would wear to my stepfather's birthday party. My mother told her where to place the pins to accentuate my waist and diminish my hips as I kept my mouth clenched, watching my small lackluster features in the mirror.

My mother sighed, addressing Alice as if I weren't there. "My

With my mother, 1965

daughter doesn't take after my side of the family. The Tolchinsky women were born with a sense of style."

"Now, now," Alice said. "Your daughter looks fine."

I bit my lip, trying not to see my reflection in the cloudy mirror. Tears were on my cheeks. I felt them welling up inside me like a geyser about to spill over. My mother began to cry too, making ugly little sounds. Alice took the pins out of her mouth and put one arm around my mother and the other arm around me. My mother leaned against Alice's shoulder.

When I was her age, my mother said, "No one ever helped me pick out a dress. My mother was always sick and too busy to notice me; she would send me to downtown Newark to shop for myself."

Alice said to me, "Honey, I think your momma's feelings are hurt because she thinks you don't love and appreciate her."

"I don't care," I muttered. The sun was making multicolored patterns on the table, and I could hear traffic on the street.

"Come on, girls," Alice said, taking us both by the hand. "Let's finish this hem." The certainty in her voice encouraged me to take off the dress and change back into my shorts. The three of us sat down on a narrow wooden sofa with embroidered cushions. The dress, which was a pink and white checked organza, cascaded across her lap. She made a few stitches along the carefully pinned hem and then handed the dress and the needle and thread to my mother who began her own delicate embroidery. "Lovely," Alice said, gently passing the dress and the needle and thread to me. I inaugurated a stitch and then another, at first gingerly and then with more confidence and ease because I knew Alice was watching me.

Tap Tap

The elevator groans like an old train as my mother and I make our way up to the fifth floor of the Ansonia hotel on the upper west side of Manhattan. We are visiting a fortuneteller named Peggy Martone, who has red hair and red lips and cheeks the color of powdery sugar. Peggy speaks just above a whisper. Her room is full of sunlight and pink brocade furniture. Greeting us in a green chiffon dress and white spike heels, she glides across the room, impersonating her younger self, a dancer in the Zigfeld Follies, who could kick high into the air and land effortlessly in a split. In the pictures on the wall, she appears as a young girl with coiffed hair and an enticing smile. In one photograph, she is wearing a huge white-feathered headdress.

Peggy is accomplished at the art of card reading. Using an ordinary deck, she casts the cards across her pink bedspread. My mother and I watch as her hands, with their short darting fingers and blood red nails, cast our fate. Hearts are for love; diamonds and clubs augur finance and spades, depending on where they fall, may bode disappointment. Peggy touches her lips with her small pink tongue. She points to a rumpled Queen of Clubs and a King of Spades and says to me, "You and your father will stay angry at each other for a long time. And I see a man; he is tall and lean and shifty-eyed. He has on a white shirt that billows like a sail. He will weave in and out of your life."

My mother and I pay Peggy, and brave the creaking elevator back down to the street. "Are cards always right?" I whisper, hoping that Peggy doesn't have supersonic hearing and isn't tuning in on our wavelength.

My mother shakes her head. "It's a matter of interpretation."

That day we buy a Ouija board, which my mother explains is a more reliable conduit to the other world than a deck of cards.

★ ★ ★

Wind taps at our living room window later that evening as my mother and I sit opposite each other on black stools with the Ouija board balanced on our laps. Dim light comes from a tall gold lamp in the corner.

My mother's expression is purposeful and a bit mischievous. "Do you want to speak to Grandma Sonia?" she quizzes me.

She means her mother, Sonia Tolchinsky, whom I've never met and has been dead for decades. I dip my head in disbelief and expectation.

The board has large black letters and numbers and a white sliding disk with a clear center which acts as a pointer. We put our fingers on the edges of the disk, and it starts to move in small concentric circles, picking up our energy.

"If we talk about your grandmother, she will come to visit," my mother suggests.

"Okay," I say. "Was she beautiful?" I ask. Faded pictures have given me only a misty view of her features.

"She had a strong face," my mother says. "Her cheekbones were high. She had soft brown eyes like yours. Her smile was slow and wise. She used to say, 'If you can't go over something and you can't go under it, go with it.'"

"What did her voice sound like?" I ask.

My mother hesitates. "It was soft and had just the hint of a Yiddish accent. My father butchered the English language, but he could read every word in an American newspaper. My mother never learned to read or write in English."

"Did she miss Russia when she came to America?"

"I'm sure she did," my mother says. "Moscow was her home. She said the buildings looked like castles in a fairy tale and in some ways her life was like a fairy tale too until she met my father and moved to Odessa. His temper was more dangerous than the pogroms in her village. He had a mistress." My mother sighs. She says, "My mother was no match for my father."

The pointer continues to move swiftly and then stops with a definitive tap on the letter Y.

My breath catches. "Does Y mean, 'Yes'? "Is Grandma Sonia here? Is she speaking to us?" I don't know if I believe what I am saying, but I like the sound of my voice giving the idea credence.

A light seems to be coming through the shadows in the room. I imagine my grandmother's face materializing in the semi-darkness.

"The night my mother died," my mother remembers, " she came to me in a dream. "She put her hand against my cheek and said, 'You're going to have a beautiful life, my darling child. I will always watch over you and keep you safe.'"

I think I see a tear on my mother's cheek. There is tightness in my chest, a sad, tender place.

We sit quietly with our knees touching while we conjure Grandma Sonia, real or imagined, to comfort us.

Parties

Kara's mother is having a party at her Greenwich Village townhouse. Kara and I are not exactly guests, but I am sleeping over, and we brush shoulders with the real guests on our way to the kitchen to get ice cream. We have on miniskirts and sway when we walk, aware of how pretty we look. Some women at the party are wearing high plastic boots and dresses that are almost see-through.

Kara's mother is an artist. Her long blond hair is streaked with gray, and she is wearing a green caftan and drinking a cocktail one small sip at a time. Her paintings hang on the walls, including portraits of Kara and her older sister, Diane, who was born with one ear and only half a face; she has had many surgeries but still doesn't look normal. Diane usually stays in her room on the second floor during parties, and most other times as well. I say hello to her when I pass her in the hallway, but I never stop to talk.

On the stereo Billie Holiday is singing a song called *Strange Fruit,* about black people being hung from trees. I know the world can be cruel and bad things can happen, but I feel insulated from all that. After the song ends, Mitch Ryder begins to sing *Devil with a Blue*

Dress On, and guests gyrate to the music. Kara and I join in, watching our pretty, young reflections in the wide windows.

From somewhere in the house, comes a hot muffled bang, and Kara's mother runs up to the second floor. Seconds later she shouts down, "Call the police?"

Diane has shot herself with a gun her mother kept in the closet. She is dead. The note she left says she was tired of being ignored because she wasn't beautiful.

Birthday Cake Dress

"Happy birthday, darling," my mother says, running a knuckle against my cheek. She heats an English muffin and lavishes it with butter and jam, just for me. At our kitchen table in Brooklyn, we sit opposite each other in the morning light, sipping coffee and talking.

"You are so young and lovely," my mother says. "I remember when I was your age." The muscles in her face tighten; her green eyes narrow, and I can tell she is seeing herself in another time and place. "My mother was already dead, so our house in Newark was dusty and quiet. My father was out with his new girlfriend, Jenny; you know the one he married."

"Did you like her?"

My mother shakes her head. "She wasn't my mother. Do you know what I did on my eighteenth birthday?"

"Yes," I say.

My mother tells the story again. "I bought myself a present and wrapped it for myself. It was a long shimmering summer dress from Bamberger's department store in downtown Newark. I tried it on in front of a full-length mirror, thinking how beautiful I looked and how lonely I felt."

My mother takes my hand and presses it. She stands up and leads me into the foyer where a box wrapped in red and white paisley paper rests on a thin yellow table. "Open it, darling. I can't wait for you to see what I got for you."

I pull off the ribbon, the paper, and the lid. A dress made of tiers of white cotton emerges. I imagine burrowing my way into it and looking like a swan, or if I'm lucky, a ballerina. The fabric is soft, and I discover a pattern of tiny embroidered stitches in the shape of stars. I press it to my cheek.

"Isn't it lovely?" my mother says. The joy and need on her face makes me afraid. I can feel her thinking. *All my love is in this dress. You must treasure it.*

"Lovely," I say. "Yes."

That evening my mother, my stepfather, and my father, whom I rarely see, along with his new wife, Annette and I go out for dinner. My friends, Kara and Brian, join us for dessert. I am wearing the dress my mother gave me, and to my surprise it falls softly around my hips and waist, making me feel pretty. A bright summer evening is at the window. The chicken is tender, but my father is not. His face is etched in angry lines. "I've almost forgotten what you look like, Steph." Since my mother's remarriage and my decision to go to high school in Brooklyn, he has regarded me as a turncoat, and I avoid him whenever I can. He laughs with a little puff of air. "Too bad you didn't get into an Ivy League college like your father, the

Harvard man."

Annette and I are wary of each other. She smiles at me, showing horse-like teeth. She smacks her silverware against her plate, and wipes her mouth in an elaborate gesture.

My mother is wearing a white silk dress that clings to her. She tosses back her head; her smile is dazzling and my father's new wife seems to shrink from it. My stepfather, decked out in a lime green suit, is talking about a court case he won fifteen years ago. My mother thrusts her chin in his direction to show that she is listening.

The following summer my stepfather will die; my mother will take a lover. My father will develop a rare blood disease and recover completely. When I fail to give him the care and attention he demands, the chasm of resentment between us will deepen. Tonight when the cake and Kara and Brian arrive, we all regard each other with forced cheer.

"Blow out the candles," my mother says. "Go ahead; make a wish."

"You're getting up there," my father says. And my stepfather chuckles in agreement. "Happy Birthday," Annette says with a slight lisp. And Kara, Brian, and I try not to giggle.

The cake is the color of my new dress and has the same lace-like pattern. There is one brilliant candle in the middle and several other smaller ones. As I stand up, I am aware everyone is watching me. I close my eyes and the room becomes dark. I feel the warmth of the candles against my cheeks. Suddenly I am flying above the table and out the window into the open sky like a figure in a Chagall painting. Kara and Brian join me, and we glide over the buildings, leaving the city and my family beneath us.

One Foot In

It is fall and the city is my college campus. In English class I am introduced to the protagonist, Raskolnikov, an impoverished student in 19th Century Russia. I follow him down a cobblestone street in St. Petersburg where he is drawn almost against his will to the flat where he had committed a murder. Through the door of another book, I ride behind Emma Bovary and her Italian lover on a field in France, feeling their lust electrify the air.

My art history professor, Miss Fielding, a young woman with a mass of red hair, tells us that art is living history. Praising the French romantic painter, Delacroix, for his expressive brush stroke, she instructs the class to make a slide in the style of his paintings. "Color and emotion should abound," she tells us.

My partner in this assignment, Sally, and I sit on black swivel stools in a coffee shop on lower Fifth Avenue, studying a museum print of *Liberty Leading the People* for inspiration. The figures in battle seem to be swaying across the canvas. A woman in a white gown stands above the living and the dead, brandishing a red flag that grazes the sky. As I look closer, I read the look on people's faces as pained and determined and imagine entering the painting, feeling the charged air.

Sally and I decide to create our own rendition of the scene. Since she has thick, dark hair that runs to her waist, soulful eyes, and a lithe frame, we decide that she will be Liberty, and I will photograph her reclining in a rowboat in Central Park in a flowing white dress and red shawl, her hair cascading against the water. The trees, the activity in the park, and the cool afternoon light will contribute to the drama of the scene.

The day I am scheduled to meet Sally by the lake it starts to rain unexpectedly. A mist comes up and the wind whistles with a fierce hum. Sally is nowhere in sight. I feel I am entering another time and place. I see a red flag waving in the distance and then Sally is running toward me, a red scarf around her neck, her hair slicked back like a matted cape.

Together we dash out of the park and up a path, where buildings line the street like a military phalanx. We take shelter under a long green canopy and watch the rain shoot silver daggers at the pavement.

"We won't get any pictures today," Sally laughs, wringing out her hair.

It is almost evening when the rain stops. A breeze circles us.

"We'd better get on the train," I say, looking at my watch. A candlelight vigil is scheduled in Bryant Park in protest against the Vietnam War. When we arrive, people are dotting the lawns, holding candles, so points of light can connect them in the growing darkness.

Sally and I join the pattern, taking candles out of our knapsacks and lighting them. I can feel an invisible cord uniting us all. What if someone were to paint us swaying defiantly in the fall air? How would we be perceived years from now? Would this moment live forever?

Seasons

Samuel and I met at an outdoor wedding in August. I remember the heat and the intense sunshine. He had a scowl on his face, and his back was bent with what I thought might be disdain. His brown hair was thick and unruly. He surprised me by taking my hand and lifting it gently as if it were a flower. "We'll see each other again," he said. I was seventeen and he was twenty-five.

Two months later on a chilly Halloween night he took me to a costume party in Greenwich Village. I wore a gold Chinese dress with a slit down the side and matching high heels decorated with synthetic sequins that sparkled. Samuel wore a military jacket and an ironic smile. I noticed the faint lines around his eyes. He told me he was writing a novel in which Moses was the main character. Because of the noise and smoke, we left the party early and wandered the narrow streets, letting the wind carry us. He took off his jacket and put it around my shoulders. I remember the weight of the jacket and the startling sense of his presence beside me as if he were a character who had leapt out of the pages of a book into my life. We sat down in a lighted coffee shop decorated with jack-o'-

lanterns and garlands of orange and black crepe paper. A small orange candle burned at our table. I remember the musty smell of rain and the way his eyes looked when he smiled, blue and alert. "I want you to be my girlfriend," he said.

It was February. Snow was falling when he, wearing high black boots and a fitted beige coat, came to pick me up. We drove to a ski resort outside the city. I remember gliding down a wide slope and thinking how tall and lean he looked as he gathered speed in front of me. Later, we sipped coffee, listening to logs crackle in a fireplace. Our legs were entwined under the table and our hands made a circle on top of the red-checkered tablecloth. I remember the shape of his thumb and the deep murmur in his throat when he said, "We'll go to Europe next summer."

With magnolia and dogwood trees in bloom, we sat close together on a narrow bench in Washington Square Park. Samuel had on jeans and a flowing white shirt. "I had to see you," he said. Arms wrapped around each other, we traversed the city. Buildings looked brazen in sunlight. Trees newly green seemed to stretch in their skins. I watched his shadow emerge on the pavement as my smaller shadow walked beside his.

Summer came again. We sat on a blanket in Central Park, not touching, listening to the swell of Mozart from the band shell. Night slid in, bringing with it a starless sky. The distance between us was palpable. He hugged his chest as if to ward off my desire for him. I watched his mouth tighten in the darkness. Months went by before he phoned again.

For years and in many seasons, he would drift in and out of my life until one March day in a café in SoHo, where jazz sounded like wild raindrops, I decided that longing was more painful than it was poignant and asked him to leave.

He flashed a slow, ironic smile. "You'll always be in my heart," he said.

Pictures on a River

I thought we would always know each other. I thought we lived in one skin. We told each other stories. Yours of a how a bullet sailed into your sister's heart while you, your brother and your mother watched. You were five. You remembered the blood inside the room and the rain outside the window, a thundering fountain. I believe you were deaf to the sound. Petrified in fear, you stood still: blue eyes wide and unseeing, faint dry lips, a tiny jaw wired for terror that would last a lifetime.

I told you how my mother came toward me like a flock of wild birds swarming into my adult life; I told you about the cruel lines around my father's mouth and his icy silence.

You could banish bad memories with the wave of your hand. Your name, James, had a magical ring to it. We would glide through the city together under skyscrapers, over the slopes of Central Park, and into the lights of Broadway.

One night during a misty spring rain, you intoned a ritual of earth, air, water, and fire. Igniting pictures from our childhoods, we cast them upon the East River, letting their stories float away with

Sunset over New York Harbor

them. I remember the scent of your breath beside me, and our laugher about any little thing, a young strong sound, tuning the city.

And now your picture floats on the river. I'm sure there were dozens of reasons why I sent you away, but I can remember only your nearness. We would sit in my small, square apartment, which faced a brick wall that cordoned off the sky and talk as if we had invented words and time. You believed in an alternate universe, the long pull of the eternal. You could inhabit almost any Shakespearean character. You could be cruel, mocking at my intonation when I read *The Love Song of J. Alfred Prufrock* aloud to you, but your barbs softened and all but disappeared over the many years I knew you.

"Of course we love each other," you would say. "We don't have to say it."

"Of course," I said, thinking this moment is everything and you are here.

Mothers and Sons

David found fault with everything, even my name. It had too many letters in it and not enough assonance. He liked things clean and spare. His studio was spacious and almost empty, and so was his apartment. As a fine arts photographer, he traveled to many parts of the country and the world in pursuit of subject matter. In a small midwestern town, he was working on a series of pictures of mothers and sons who lived together for life. The sons wore ragged jeans; their eyes were wide and vacant. The mothers, who appeared thick and languid, refused to look directly at the camera. He captured their shapeless floral print dresses and their fat black shoes. Many of the pictures were taken in black and white. The spaces between the mothers and sons seemed endless and dull, as if no words or light or air had ever entered their homes. One son had a pendant of a cow around his neck, which lay against his rumpled shirt. These were not my favorite series of his photographs, but I admired his artistry. I liked the pictures of a female bareback rider on a tall white horse posed against the sky on the Coney Island boardwalk.

Often I didn't like him. The pictures he took of me reflected the most somber aspect of my personality, as if his camera were a critical eye designed to accentuate my flaws. David wanted to rearrange my wardrobe and my ideas. He dressed in flagrant rebellion against the conventional, his clothing and hair in disarray. He snickered at my sensible shoes. On the subway he would sneer at men and women in business suits as if they were monkeys in a cage of respectability. "In your heart you're like them," he would say.

Despite our differences, there were tender moments between us. I remember the walk across the promenade in Brooklyn Heights when the Twin Towers were still standing and late afternoon sun filtered like gold around them. We walked fast as if we were walking on water. At dusk we wandered the streets of Brooklyn Heights, stopping in front of a lighted bookstore. I remember the large hardback books in the window with titles in red letters. Standing behind me, he put his arms around my waist. There was no space between us. I was aware only of my soft leather jacket and his touch. What if we could have stayed liked that with the hooked moon above us and our fear and distrust in the shadows behind us, our mothers' voices transmuted into rational thought: *Everyone will betray you sooner or later. You will never leave me.*

Returning Things

My mother dies so gently. Her breath slows like summer air. She turns her palms up, a small, heroic gesture and then she is gone. I carry this good feeling to her funeral, providing the rabbi with a list of her virtues: emotional strength, a keen intelligence, a powerfully creative aesthetic.

Yet in the months following her death anger begins to flicker and then flair as vivid, indignant memories force their way to the surface.

I am eight years old, and it is early fall; I am being dragged along a wide Manhattan street. A mean wind whistles in my ear as my mother shouts, "I will never forgive you for all the things you've done to me." I make my body rigid; my vision blurs. I think I see her white blond hair make a frame for her face. There is a scream inside of me.

When I am sixteen, she forces herself into my room while I am dressing; her eyes are alight with cruelty. I shiver. "It takes guts to wear black pants and brown shoes. Doesn't it, kid?" She smoothes the folds of her leopard-print dress. Her smile is a scornful crescent. "You will never be half the woman I am," she says.

* * *

"I love you," my mother said on the telephone year after year and then waited for the obligatory, "I love you too." I gave it to her dutifully, not seeing an alternative. She had my complicity in our secret—love was roughed in hate, shame and blame; it was the witch's finger coated in sugar, beckoning. I want to give that love back altogether.

And what of the touch of her hand on my cheek on a childhood morning? Will I have to return that love too? Or will the crust of my hatred for her fall away, so love can pass from world to world?

Traveling

My students, many of them designers from Asia, Europe and Africa, take me around the world with them in their narratives. Summer sun hits a Japanese farm as my student, Keiko, who is six years old, is watching her grandmother work. She likes the older woman's lean back and her long hands that turn up the earth with a quiet majesty. Her grandmother is standing far away from her, and Keiko can see her wide-brimmed hat with a string under the chin that looks as if it were painted there.

    Her grandmother is not a sweet grandma; her kitchen and her thoughts are orderly, and she tells Keiko what to do in a cold, calm voice. Sometimes she thinks she sees a smile in her grandmother's eyes. Keiko imagines running up to her, and throwing her arms around her legs, and planting a kiss on her tan, wrinkled cheek. Her grandma wears a burlap shoulder bag when she works, and in it she keeps a wallet made of woven straw. The autumn Keiko turns ten her grandmother slips quietly out of life, and is buried in the earth she loves. Keiko, now a woman of twenty, carries the burlap shoulder bag with her as if it were a part of her skin; the wallet inside it is stiff and tender, the way she remembers her grandmother.

My student, Emma, takes me to Italy, where she and her fiancé scale a winding mountain road on a motorbike to Monte Cassini, a hilltop monastery made of white brick. On the hilltop the ground is flat, and doves land gently on pillars; the atmosphere is peaceful and quiet, yet Emma's thoughts are not. She is afraid marrying Jon will limit her options. She envisions her apartment in New York, which is also her studio, with her patterns on display on every chair and table. Will there be room for a husband and children? Will Jon try to persuade her to live in a small Italian village? Emma wants to run into the shadows of the pillars as Jon walks toward her, his hands raised in supplication, a questioning look on his face.

My student Sigrid tells of her mad dash across a field in Estonia, which leads her to trip and fall to the bottom of a well. She is three-years-old, and the walls of the well echo with her cries; above her she thinks she sees a patch of sky; her mother comes and pulls her to safety; this experience teaches her to watch and wait and believe she can overcome anything.

On JeJu Island in Korea my student Jung and her father stand above the sea, which sways with hypnotic circular ease. Jung's father, a stern and shy man who has always encouraged her to find what is important in her life, turns to her with his long face and dark eyes and says, "Go to America. Follow your dream." His words seem to write themselves on the water.

I walk behind my student in a desert in Israel. He is a captain in the army on a practice mission. He is in love with the night, the way the sky and the sea seem to trade places under the moon, and the wind blows like a wild dog, holdings its breath and then letting it out in snarling gusts. The sand is cool as we find our way back to the army post in Tel Aviv.

In China my student Yi is studying her image in a full-length mirror. Her dress, which just reaches her knee, has a silver pattern of trees and flowers on a pink background, accentuating its elegance and hers. The high and tight collar forces her to raise her chin. She is a confident Chinese lady, ready for anything. This traditional Chinese qípáo is the last gift she has given herself before embarking on a four-year trip to America. Complex desires well up inside her like threads she wants to draw together. She is going to a strange country to seek independence, yet she is also determined to represent herself as a Chinese woman and honor her family and country. The new and the old come back to her in her reflection: a modern girl in a classic dress. She is like China, growing up fast, yet keeping what is historically and traditionally precious. "Thank you, qípáo," she says aloud to the dress. "I will always carry you with me and remember I am Chinese."

My student Victoria invites me to her elementary school in the Soviet Union in 1989, a few years before its demise. I discover spacious corridors; on one side of the hallway there are numerous doors, and on the other a wall of windows; children squint in early spring sunlight as they run happily out of class. Victoria, and her friend Sasha, and hundreds of other students pour down the stairs; their footsteps sound like joyous thunder. They are wearing brown dresses, and black aprons, and badges with images of Lenin on them. Spring instills a spirit of adventure in both girls, and they decide to navigate buses and trains to Sasha's house in the countryside. The sky is dark when they arrive, and Victoria realizes her family doesn't know her whereabouts. When she arrives home that night to confront her mother's exhaustion and her sister's scared eyes, she realizes that love restricts freedom, even in the Soviet Union, which she has been taught to believe is the safest and best country in the world.

In another house in Russia some years later, my student Patti and her family struggle to put out a fire in a coal-burning stove. When flames continue to leap in orange rage, the family manages to escape through the door into a world of thick winter snow. Even the sky is white with cold. I hear voices on the wind that seem reminiscent of another century. They are low and guttural as a cry, and I sense they belong to my maternal grandfather and great-grandfather. I follow them to a small house on a limestone street. Wind is blowing over the sea and knocking against the windows. I press my head against the glass, watching and listening.

PART IV

Family History

Grandpa Joseph's Suit

The rain has stopped. Sunlight comes uninvited through the windows of my maternal grandfather Joseph's house in Odessa. He and his sister Mina are sitting on a long, narrow wooden bench, their eyes cast downward at the floor. Joseph, who is twelve, is dressed in a black suit, too large for him. The suit, a hand-me-down from his cousin Isaac, has been pressed so many times that the threads gleam. Mina has on a brown dress; her blond hair is plaited around her head. Suddenly brother and sister touch hands and turn toward one another, seeking out each other's faces.

Their mother Rebecca, a thin woman with a round face, stands hidden in the folds of a black cape; her dark eyes are desolate. Tall and broad shouldered, their father, Max, taps his cane in a gesture of authority. His voice sounds like an insistent drum. "Sit up straight," he commands his son. Joseph stretches in his suit, trying to find the dimensions of his body. The jacket, which buttons at the throat, falls almost to his knees. The worn pants, rolled up at the cuffs, threaten to unravel.

"Come this way," his father says. Father and son walk into the parlor, where neighbors, speaking in hushed voices, weave back and forth in front of a small wooden box. The sound of a violin wafts through the house, and Joseph can feel the music inside him, tantalizing him with its mournful beauty. He is at his nine-year-old brother Simka's funeral. Simka's cheeks are painted white by death. He is wearing a white nightshirt; his lips appear dry and tender. Joseph wants to take off his jacket and fold it around Simka as a blanket his younger brother can take with him to another world. The sound of his father's cane stops him. His suit seems to swallow him up and draw him into its flimsy armor. He is sure the buttons will never come undone, and he will be trapped forever in ill-fitting darkness. He unbuttons the top button and then the next, breathing hard as if he had been running. He lets the jacket fall over his shoulders and onto the floor as Max moves toward him. When the jacket touches the ground, father and son watch it turn into a prayer shawl stitched with gold thread. Max's breath catches in his chest; he lets his cane fall to the ground. Gently Joseph lifts the shawl and places it over his brother's body.

Mina's Braids

At six my grandfather Joseph is in love with the spring air. He has cherries in his pockets that smell like strong perfume. He puts one in his mouth and licks it whole and sweet, wanting to delay biting into it. The sun beats down on his head, and makes him feel dizzy. He stops where the sun parts two trees and the ground is a thin floor of dirt. He hears a rustling sound and a sob. He sees his father, Max, pulling his sister Mina across the ground by her long blond braids. "You disobeyed me!" Max shouts.

Joseph leaps toward his father and sister, trying to wrestle Mina free. Max shoves Joseph and Mina to the ground and stands above both his children. His arms are long and languorous like the appendages of a giant spider. He picks up his cane, which has been resting against a tree, and smacks it against the ground. The sky goes black, and there is only the rush of wind in my grandfather Joseph's ear.

Joseph finds himself in his narrow bed with night at the window. The moon brings light into the room. His mother sits next to him, a look of concern on her face. She strokes his forehead, and her hand feels like a worn cloth that is gentle and familiar. "Sleep now," she says. "You've had a bad dream."

Father and Son

———————

At sixteen-years-old, my grandfather Joseph stands small in his work overalls. His lips are curled in concentration. With a thick needle, he is sewing the arm of a leather vest. Each thrust is precise; the leather is challenging, brown and humbly soft. He stands above a sturdy wooden table; the vest rests against it as he works on it. Suddenly the needle snaps, giving way at its neck. He will have to get another from a neighbor boy named Nicolas, who has a raucous laugh, and carries stones in his pocket that he can make dance on water.

A sudden burst of light narrows my grandfather's vision as his father, Max, enters the barn, where he is working. Joseph is aware of his father's towering presence as the older man advances toward him. The cane, which his father acquired five years ago after a fall, appears to his son as a weapon. Max stops in front of the table, surveying the vest; his mouth turns down at the corners with disdain.

He laughs a hard, dry laugh as he regards Joseph. "You will never amount to anything," he says. "This is obvious. Look at these stitches.

You are a useless fool."

    Joseph feels the blood beat at his temples. Shame tastes like stale bread in his mouth. Will he meet his father's eyes? He turns toward the window, where lemony-yellow light defines the sky. There are particles of dust everywhere. He sees an ox-drawn carriage meander down the street. Joseph looks back up at his father, forcing a defiant gaze. Max's face begins to soften. He takes a step forward, putting a hand on Joseph's shoulder. There is gruff affection in his voice. "You are my son. Make me proud of you."

What is America?

My great grandfather, Max, slaps his cane against the hard Russian earth. "Joseph," he says to his son. "You must go to America. There is danger here."

Joseph feels his chest swell with pride. He has been chosen to write a new chapter in the life of his family. It is summer and father and son are in the park where the trees are thick with leaves. Joseph lets air into his lungs and then out again with a deep sigh.

His father steps toward him. "You can make a new life and bring our family there."

Joseph hears his own thoughts like an excited drum before they become words; his voice jumps out with a big, brash sound. "I will go to America, Papa."

But what is America? Joseph can't see it; he can't hear it; he can't smell it. It is just a foreign land on a map that promises honey. He sees himself sailing on a ship with the mast touching the stars; he feels the swell of the sea under the belly of the ship and feels the wind as a thousand whips knotted together, moving the ship forward, away from everything he knows. Suddenly the Russian soil feels like sacred ground. He wants to pick up a fist full of dirt and press it against his cheeks. He wants the hills and the river to rise up and greet him. He wants to join the circle of earth, sea, and sky. How can he leave his city and his country? Wouldn't he be leaving himself?

Sensing his son's indecision, his father shouts, "Joseph, you will go to America."

And my grandfather nods his head in assent. Around him the sky is alive with the rich, pink glow of afternoon; it will be there in America and so will he.

In Six Days

The space is a gutted shell with sawdust everywhere. It is the lack of any shape and the dust and the thick air that make my grandfather Joseph want to run. He is waiting for his partner, Saul Mandelbaum, and this wreck of a building is the home for a supermarket they will construct rack by rack with cans of beans and vegetables and paper goods and flour. The Jews of Newark, exported from Russia, will spill inside with coins in their hands.

The windows of the supermarket will be dressed with enticing fruit: plastic apples so real looking the neighborhood kids will long to bite into them. Mandelbaum is a wizard when it comes to money; he knows how to make it stretch. A dollar becomes ten. But it is he, Joseph, who has the imagination to make this place hum with warmth and nourishment.

He looks out the window, which is smudged and wide, and overlooks Chancellor Avenue. Snow is piled high, and kids in black snow boots are dragging wooden sleds up a hill. Shivering in his wool shirt, my grandfather grabs a broom from the corner with a hard, determined motion and begins to shove the debris into the

My grandfather, Joseph Tolchinsky, circa 1922

middle of the room. Fresh snow has begun to fall against the window, fading the sky. The world around him is growing dim. He plows through the wreckage as if it were everything that ever stood in his way. His young body is agile; he is sure he can fly. He doesn't hear Mandelbaum's key turn in the lock. If God could make the world in six days, he can run a supermarket.

The Ghost of Papa Max

Max is here. Joseph is almost sure of it. His father has been dead for a year, yet his energy fills the air. In his bedroom in Newark, Joseph thinks he can hear a whistle, or is it only the sound of the wind moving the curtains?

His wife Sonia lies next to him. Her body is soft and pliable. A street light outside their window shines on them both, and Joseph imagines caressing his wife the way the light does, touching her shoulder, her left breast, and the curve of her hip. He will take the hairpins out of her bun and let her dark hair fall across his pillow.

An ancient cold slides over the bed. "God damn you!" he says to his father in his heart. "What do you want?"

The air around him is becoming clearer, and he thinks he sees points of light in the darkness. Fingertips are touching his temples. As a cold hand finds the small of his back and lingers there, Joseph can feel his wife's warm touch over his heart. Her gentle breath calms him as she whispers, "Be hospitable, Joseph; your father is paying us a visit."

On Friday Nights

It is Friday night in my grandmother's kitchen. Sitting at the head of the table, she wears a lace prayer shawl over her fine dark hair, which is pulled back in a bun. She fills the folds of her white cotton dress like a monument to patience. Lighting the Sabbath candles, she murmurs a prayer in a voice so low it could enter another sphere. She presses her full lips against one another; her face is illuminated by candlelight; her dark eyes shine. Her back is broad; her hips are wide; she has given birth to five children, all of them grown except for my mother; three of them are here tonight.

My aunt Rose sits to her mother's right. She is a tall woman with ink-black hair and long tapered fingers. Her husband, Abe, has forsaken her for life on a houseboat in Florida, where the current carries him away from his law practice and his family, unheard of for a Jewish husband. Rose is passionate about Abe's bitter smile, the way it pulls his cheek to the right, and the birthmark on the palm of his left hand that is as indelible as her love for him. He will come back to her; she is sure of it. Her mother has warned Rose against passion, the underwater dance from which one may never emerge, but Rose is ripe for the thorns of love.

Her daughter, Anna, who at twelve has a sultry glare, sits next to her mother. Rose pinches her daughter's thigh. "Sit up," she directs. And Anna, who longs to throw an arsenal of plates at her mother, complies. She feels a smile forming behind her somber face. Later, in her room, she will watch herself become Ava Gardner in the mirror. She will pull her sweater tightly across her chest and let her tongue linger over her bottom lip. There is a world of men waiting for her.

My uncle Nathan, who is sitting next to Anna, folds into a parody of himself. Long and lean as Errol Flynn, he is in love with his handsome face and dark hair; women are too. His wife Betty beats them off with her fists when they knock at her door, drunk and calling for my uncle's blood, demanding from him a commitment he has never promised.

My grandfather Joseph sits opposite his wife. He appears stiff and erect behind his perfect bowtie; his face resembles the painted face of the man on the herring jars he sells in his grocery store. He has grown out the fringes of his hair and meticulously combed them over the crown of his head to conceal its bald center. His blue eyes are wide and luminous; they twinkle. He reveres his wife, yet he is thinking of his mistress, Mimi. He sighs, hoping to escape later tonight to her apartment on Girard Street, where shadows will usher him into the folds of her body. He sees her silhouette in the eye of the candle his wife is lighting.

My grandmother raises her head from the effort of prayer and smiles at her family. It is a gentle smile, a gathering of all her goodwill. She is determined to give legitimacy to this profligate group.

My mother sits to her mother's right. At thirteen she has crimson lips, white skin and auburn hair, which falls to her shoulders in waves. She is "a true beauty" her Papa is fond of saying. While boys and girls pursue her, she prefers the company of books; they are worlds she can enter, becoming Joan of Arc, Guinevere in King Arthur's court, or Queen Elizabeth the First as a young woman with flaming red hair, commanding a nation. Tonight she is fully present, reveling in her mother's attention. As my grandmother regards her youngest daughter, a painful feeling stirs in her heart. She who must give so much to so many people has only a small ration of love left. My grandmother raises her hand to my mother's cheek and strokes it gently.

Fire in Moscow

My grandfather Joseph sleeps like a stone, while my grandmother Sonia lies awake, eyes wide with remembrance. She and her mother are walking down a Moscow street. Sonia is twelve and her mother, Henny, a tall, redheaded woman, towers over her. Around them, buildings look like clouds that have congealed into stone. They will meet her father, Peter, and other concerned citizens on the second floor of a synagogue to discuss the attacks on Jewish villages. As they walk, they see armed security police and workers waving banners in protest. Henny grips her daughter's arm when they turn a corner.

In the distance Sonia notices smoke gathering; red flames singe a building, taking it by the roots like a coil of fire. She feels the smoke thicken and dust begin to fly; the air is no longer distinguishable from the sky. She starts to cough and choke and her mother's hand falls away from her. She is alone, fighting for air. A siren shrieks by her. She runs as fast as her feet will carry her to where she can see a patch of blue sky. The air is clearer as buildings take shape like domed castles; the street is wide and unfamiliar. Trees bow their heads to greet her. She sees a small girl in a black coat, gripping her mother's hand as if it were a prize.

Sonia remembers her own mother. Was Henny consumed by smoke? Did she dash down another street where the wind carried her to safety? Sonia's thoughts swirl inside her for a moment. What if she never were to see her mother again? Her mother, who wears black dresses with white lace collars; her mother, whose voice sounds like chimes clashing together; her mother, whose hands are almost as white as marble; her mother who doesn't love her as much as she loves her sister, Tanya, whose magnificent dark braid falls to her waist. What if she were to walk into the house of another family where the mother wore an apron made of lace and offered her sweets on a silver tray? What if she were to disappear into a new life?

The Shawl

Sonia's shawl is made of delicate white lace. She loves the way it falls over her shoulders and wraps her in its elegance. It is a gift from her father, Peter, who says she looks like a Russian princess in it. When she wears the shawl, she holds her head up high and imagines a crown has been placed on it by a member of her court, an arc of diamonds that sparkles when she walks.

When her mother shouts at her or shows disdain, she imagines the shawl is part of her skin and stands strong and tall, lifting her chin and raising her voice to defend herself.

Her mother takes notice of Sonia's new stance. One day in the parlor, Henny walks up to her daughter with the beginning of a smile on her face. "Sonia dear, would you like some tea?" The two women sit opposite each other at a small table covered with a lace cloth. The amber liquid in their glasses mixes with the sunlight at the window. They regard each other with curiosity and affection.

Sonia is wearing the shawl the night she meets my grandfather, Joseph, at a dance. He and his father have come to Moscow from Odessa to discuss the problem of the pogroms with men like her father, Peter, who want to keep their country safe for the Jews. Joseph is short yet gallant; his black hair forms a cap on his head. His mustache is carefully brushed. Music falls around them as they begin to spin in a synchronized motion across the floor.

Sonia wears the shawl on her wedding day. It blends perfectly with her lace gown, which falls over her hips so gently she feels as if she could float in space. Her mother and sister have helped her prepare for the occasion; her cousin, Lila, a seamstress, has altered her dress, taking it in at the waist, letting the high, white bodice give shape to her chest and throat.

Sonia studies her reflection in a mirror in the anteroom before the ceremony. Her brown hair is piled in a luxurious bun. Her wide lips narrow in a kind of repose. Joseph will take her away from Moscow to Odessa, where, he tells her, the light is golden and the ocean swells in thick, whipped-cream-like foam. Yet a light in Joseph's eyes frightens her; his penetrating blue gaze hardens when something displeases him. Will he be cruel to her? Will his thin lips open to emit words he will regret saying? Will the magic between them survive the wheel of daily life? Will a shawl really protect her from all that might happen?

There is a weight on Sonia's chest, pressing down hard like a warning. In the mirror, she sees her older self materialize; her face appears round and lined; there is pain and regret in her brown eyes. She bows her head, forcing herself back to the present. The music swells and she hears her sister Tanya's voice, bustling and efficient, calling to her. "Come, Sonia. Hurry. The ceremony is starting."

The Train Station

Marina Talinskaya, the daughter of Abram and Miriam Talinskaya, has been killed in a train accident, traveling with her family from Moscow to St. Petersburg. Her body, clad in boots and a dark coat, was found on the tracks.

His voice thick with emotion, my grandmother Sonia's father, Peter, is reading to his family from a newspaper.

The news of her friend's death makes her breath feel like a small thing. She can hear the train thundering over Marina's body; she can see the engine's harsh head of steam. Were Marina's bones crushed like a bird's?

That night in the room she shares with her sister my grandmother closes her eyes and envisions Marina's long blond hair, her bright blue eyes, and the freckles on her cheeks. She sees the two of them running in their long winter coats, laughing and looking around them at a white fairytale world.

A sparkling of dust appears in the night, and she thinks she hears Marina's soft familiar voice saying, "Go to the train station tomorrow after school. I will meet you there."

Yet the following afternoon when Sonia arrives, a train has just departed, and she encounters only lonely tracks and gray sky. "I will never forget you, Marina Talinskaya," she says, feeling the sting of cold on her cheeks.

A strong wind comes up around her, and a voice inside her head seems to be speaking to her. "You will travel across an ocean and live in a new country," the voice says. "This is certain."

At sixteen, Sonia has no intention of leaving Russia. Suddenly she wants to wrap the sky around her. Moscow is the air she breathes, and the food she eats. She pictures the hills and winding streets that abruptly begin and end, posing continual mystery. She remembers the way her bed creaks and sees the small wooden chair in her room with a crack down the middle. She feels the excitement of dark winter nights lighted only by mist and stars. "I will never leave Russia," she says to anyone living or dead who might be listening.

Now thirty years later, residing in Newark, with her husband and children, the sights, and the sounds of her native country are as palpable as they were when she was a girl. In America, her husband's temper as well as his tenderness, the long hours working by his side in the grocery store, her children coming one after another with their own needs and desires, crowding out her thoughts, have never been as real to her as her early life in Moscow.

Running Wild in Newark

It is snowing in Newark. Chancellor Avenue is covered with a fine white coat as my mother, who is almost twelve years old, bounds down the street. She is in love with Christmas even though her parents are pious Jews, who would never even entertain the idea of getting her a tree that glitters with red and gold lights and has garlands of silver tinsel and a star on top. At home her mama will soon light the Chanukah candles with solemn and delicate hands, explaining how important it is to honor the plight of the ancient Jews who crossed a desert to freedom. My mother thinks the menorah has magical fingers of light, but she can't help picturing a Christmas tree in the corner, fragrant and green and dazzling.

The snow is falling faster as she reaches downtown Newark, where a trolley car glides down the wide street, and people armed in coats and scarves maneuver about, doing their Christmas shopping. The windows of Bamberger's department store are decorated with plump Christmas wreaths and giant candy canes. In one window, a Santa in a red suit and hat, smiles at her, and my mother can't help smiling back.

The wind carries her around a corner, almost lifting her and dropping her down on the falling snow. She ducks into a red brick building, where her Hebrew class is being held, and slips into a brown wooden desk next to her friend, Helen Goodfellow, a twelve-year-old who wears a bra and has a crush on a gentile boy named Gil Masterson. The girls smile at each other, pretending a show is about to start in which their teacher, Mr. Goldmeister, will be the star. My mother is not his favorite pupil because she asks questions that threaten the moral rectitude of the bible like, "After Adam and Eve had Cain and Abel, where did the rest of the people come from?" Today she flashes him a mischievous smile.

Mr. Goldmeister rubs his hands together and explains that Moses had the honor of speaking to God on many occasions and that God invested him with the power to make the Red Sea part so that the Jews could walk across it. A boy named Adam raises his hand to offer what he thinks is scientific evidence to the contrary, but Mr. Goldmeister waves him away. He opens a small bottle of red ink and pours it across his desk to demonstrate the challenge Moses had faced. He raises his hand in a dramatic gesture, knocking over the inkwell and sending sticky red ink and splinters of glass across the table and onto the floor. As Mr. Goldmeister searches for a cloth to clean up the mess, my mother winks at Helen and puts her coat back on.

In minutes she is outside, catching snowflakes in her mouth and following the blue glaze of winter. She runs past Mr. Solomon's tailor shop, where the windows are dark. He has closed early for the

Sabbath. She loves his gentle smile, even his gold front teeth, and the fact that he lets her help him sew on buttons and finish hems. The snow is falling even harder, and Newark has become a misty, white world. Tomorrow the streets will be covered with black sludge, but today nothing can take away its beauty.

My mother doesn't go to her house because she knows her Mama won't be missing her. When my mother was a little girl, her mother and father worked side by side in the grocery store. But then her Mama's kidneys started to ache, so her Papa sent her home, where she began to confiscate dust and polish furniture with an ardor that presupposed the safety of her family and the world depended on the order she would achieve. By this time in the afternoon, my mother knows her mother is sitting at the cream-colored kitchen table, drinking tea out of a glass and talking with their neighbor, Mrs. Worstel, about the fact that men can't be trusted.

She is sure that her papa is in his store, sweeping the floor with zeal, and then looking up and marveling at the shiny cans on his shelves, and the glass jars of herring that are all his. He has placed a menorah and a paper loaf of challah in the window. There are also reindeer and a Santa Claus put there to accommodate the Irish and Italian families who have heard Joseph Tolchinsky has the best cake in Newark.

The wind pushes her right in front of her father's store window and forces her to stop. As she looks inside, the atmosphere appears foggy and dreamlike. Her father has on a thick red shirt, and his hair stands out like a wild halo around his head. He is behind the cash register, and she can almost hear the clattering of the keys and the drawer opening and closing as she watches him.

She pulls open the big wooden door and steps inside. When her father spots her, his mouth curves in a smile. "My princess," he says. "My darling girl." He is her sweet papa today. Not the papa who tells her she is an ugly, stupid girl. Not the papa with a growl in his voice that brings icy fear to her stomach. Not the papa, who pulls her by the hair and threatens to send her to a home for retarded people.

"Come," he says. "Help me decorate these windows, my little genius." My mother watches her father's eyes light on her as if she were his prize possession. There is genuine happiness on his face. She walks slowly, carefully toward him, so as not to break the spell.

Transgressions

Her sister Aida's shoes hang from the wall from a thick nail. My mother strokes the soft brown leather; she takes in their scent. With their cutaway sides and open toes, they appear to be so petite and springy that in them she could walk on air. Would they fit her ten-year-old feet?

Aida is ten years older than my mother, and the mother of two fat, blue-eyed boys; she has come home to live, after Dave, her husband of five years, took a mistress in South Orange, a woman, Aida says, with platinum blond hair, a squeaky voice, and pink nails like gum drops.

It is Aida who takes my mother shopping. The big gold doors of Bamberger's department store swing open for them, and they ride the escalator to the third floor, where Aida picks out dresses and coats and shoes for my mother. My mother thinks about the blue wool coat with brass buttons she got last winter that makes her feel so grown-up.

Her own mother never takes her shopping. Her kidneys ache, and she is often tired. The house on Chancellor Avenue is her domain. The floors gleam and the pots sparkle; she lets ingredients fall into them in magical sequence. The thick aroma of kreplach permeates the air. The family gravitates to her table as they would to an oasis. Even her papa tears himself away from his mistress Lena's soft white flesh to enjoy his wife's cooking.

Since Aida is a grown woman, she helps her mother in the kitchen, cutting, shaping, molding, and baking while they scoot my mother away. *You are too small and clumsy to enter our world* she hears them think as she runs off, making loud steps on the floor, which is polished to a harsh shine.

Her mama never has time for her; they never buy dresses together or share secrets. Aida has her mama, and she doesn't.

My mother takes Aida's shoes off the nail and slips them on her feet. They almost fit. She runs down the wooden staircase and into the spring air, feeling the pavement under the soles as she picks up speed. *Stolen,* she thinks as she sprints down the street.

Grandma Sonia's Funeral

Sunlight is coming through the window. It is a burnt color, a bleeding yellow light. My mother is sitting toward the front of the temple on a hard wooden bench; the rabbi is speaking in a deep, resonant voice.

"Sonia Tolchinsky was a pious woman, a woman of charity, simplicity and grace. She was a devoted wife and mother and sister and friend. She was beloved and revered by all who knew her."

My mother, who is fourteen, breathes in the praise about her mother as if it were strong perfume. Her older sister Aida sits beside her; Aida is a mother herself of two fat boys that wrap themselves around her like elves, as well as the estranged wife of a philandering husband. Lost in grief, Aida dabs her eyes with a tissue and does not comfort my mother.

Solemn and mute, my mother's father sits behind her, next to his sister, Mina. My mother's eldest sister, Rose, is wearing a black hat with a wide brim; sorrow elongates her face. Her daughter, Anna, sits next to her, fidgeting with her skirt. My mother's brothers, Nathan and Phil, are wearing black suits and somber gray ties. There

My grandmother, Sonia Tolchinsky, circa 1936

are other relatives in the room whom my mother recognizes, and many people she doesn't know.

The bench is hard, where she sits in her plain, brown dress, which she has chosen because she knows her mother would have found it appropriate. My mother prefers colors that flash and shout, colors louder than the colors of the rainbow. Her mother's voice was soft, and she has the beginning of a bark and a whistle in hers. The rabbi is talking. He has a round face and small eyes and only a touch of color as if the sun had burned two red spots around his mouth, so people would pay attention when he spoke.

"Sonia Tolchinsky's generosity was magnificent. Right here in this room there are families she quietly supported for years, giving them clothes and food. They live and breathe the good air because of this good woman."

Having her mother portrayed in saintly terms gives my mother a funny tickle in her throat. The sun comes in the window more clearly and with it the scent of spring. Is her mother really gone? Did she ever really live? My mother tries to etch an image of her mother in her mind. She sees sad dark eyes and a thick neck and white hands that are afraid to unfold themselves.

My mother clasps her own hands together, one hand supporting the other, and waits for the rabbi to finish.

Girl on a Pony

At fourteen, after her mother's death, my mother searches for her younger self in pictures. She finds herself at seven in pale green shorts and a matching shirt, sitting on a pony in front of a yellow house. Both she and the pony appear to be inordinately still. My mother's eyes are expressionless; she is neither looking at the camera nor away from it.

She remembers the day the picture was taken. There was a gray sky and summer trees in the distance. She can feel her desire to freeze time. Her father is walking toward her. He puts a hand on her waist; her breath is trapped in her chest and flutters there.

"Sit up straight and smile," he says. "You look like a retarded fool with your mouth hanging open."

My mother blinks and breathes; the air around her seems to gather smoke; she imagines the sky is a shield between her father and herself. He leans closer to her, letting his lips touch her ear. "Stupid, ugly girl," he laughs. And it is a laughter that settles into her skin.

As her father walks away from her, my mother shifts in the saddle and the pony moves with her. The photographer hides behind a black cape and lights explode like shooting stars.

Her Lover

Her lips, outlined in red, cast a shadow against her white skin. She has on silk stockings with black seams down the back. My mother is waiting for her lover, Arthur, a French-Canadian, whose dark hair falls over his left eye. She thinks of his long tapered fingers and his voice that rises and falls as imperceptibly as a river and always leaves her wanting more.

She is at a train station. She and Arthur will be traveling to Vancouver; he is late as usual. The steel train before her has the quality of an inert monster. She looks at her watch.

She entices herself with the memory of a previous vacation. Last summer she and Arthur were on a Long Island beach, where the sand was cool silk and Arthur's lips were at the nape of her neck. As a wave broke, she turned toward him and his mouth became part of the sky on her throat, her shoulders, and her cheeks. His hand on her back was the sea itself, tugging her down to the sand.

She saw faces in the darkness carved out of sand and sky: an irate father, a future jealous husband, her younger self in awe of her abandon.

The wind cuts through her stockings and stings her cheeks. She checks her watch. She will not board the train without him. She feels small and lost under the winter sky.

My Mother and My Father

My mother has on a peasant blouse that falls over her shoulders. Her long brown hair curves in gentle waves. Her skin is pale; her lips are cherry red; her green eyes are cast down at her feet where she wears beige leather high-heeled shoes. Her skirt is sun-colored. As I look closely at the photograph, I notice that her brow is knit as if by inner concerns. There is a shy almost frightened light in her eyes.

My father stands next to her in a thick, yellow shirt, wearing a camera-ready smile. Behind them there are palm trees and Florida sunshine. I am three months old and at home with a babysitter. My trenchant cries have caused them to escape to a place where they can have uninterrupted time together.

When I look closely at the photograph, I see that my mother's eyes are slanted toward my father's chest; his dark eyes are watching her with adulation. Love is the signature in this faded image. Their hands touch in a kind of unity of purpose. They will build a life, raise a child, watch the sky together, and dream of greatness.

The photograph is streaked down the middle, giving them both

My mother and my father, Florida, circa 1951

a separate space. Their shoulders aren't quite touching; they are close yet straining away from each other.

Mirror Mirror

At thirty-five, my mother stands in front of the mirrored wall in her dressing room. She is wearing a form-fitting black dress embroidered with tiny sequins. Her hair is a blond bouffant; her lips are a pale pink. Light rouge highlights her prominent cheekbones. She is living alone in a small Manhattan apartment enlivened by her sense of style. She luxuriates in the space around her. Her father died of a heart ailment the summer before; she is divorced from my father, and I am living in a boarding school in New Jersey. She has no one to answer to.

My mother enjoys watching the strong contours of her own face. Her chin is sharp and decisive. Tonight she will go to the opera with a man named Harrison, a physician who admires her beauty and enjoys her company. Yet she is in no rush to make him or any man her new husband.

She has her own dreams. She imagines her line of dresses being displayed in well-known department stores in Paris, Milan, and New York City. To cultivate her intellect, she will earn a law degree and become a criminal attorney. Her knowledge of history and politics will come alive in the courtroom. She envisions herself standing before a jury in a gray tailored suit, offering cogent arguments in her client's defense.

My father had often scoffed at her intelligence, telling her that she was all pout and fluff, and no match for the mind of a Harvard man. Her own father, even when she was an adult, had called her his helpless baby doll. She is no one's doll or baby now. The lights around the dressing room mirror give a glow to her cheeks. For a moment she can feel the thrum of greatness inside her.

Yet as she studies her reflection more carefully, her eyes appear too wide and her smile too bright. She is aware of the coldness in the room. Crude and uninvited, self-doubt encroaches upon her.

Bound for Greatness

When my father was seven, he and his family made a trip across the ocean from Russia to America. I imagine him disembarking from the ship as if it were the Ark, walking next to his father, a stern man with high cheekbones and a dismissive manner. "Stand up straight, Louie," he said, "and don't whimper." His flamboyant, red-haired mother came next with her two younger children: his sister Sara, who kept looking at the sky, and his brother, Phil, who was small and square.

Their first home was a tenement on Manhattan's Lower East Side, where my father, who missed the open sky of Odessa, wanted to knock down the low stone buildings to see what was behind them. At night, seeing the fire of the pogroms in his dreams, he would cry in his sleep. His mother would put a cool cloth to his head and his father would say, "Weak boy. Remember you're a man."

On Saturday mornings, while his mother attacked the family clothes on a scrub board, she would turn to my father and whisper, half in Yiddish and half in English, low enough so that the others couldn't hear. "Louie, you're my special little boy. You're going to make a mark in the world."

My father felt a smile grow on his face. He knew he was smart; he could make the English language sound like music.

"Forget the old country," his mother had said. "You are an American. No one has to know where you come from."

A few years later when the family had moved to Staten Island and his father was selling two-story dwellings, my father washed his Russian heritage away like a thin layer of grime. For the rest of his life he told everyone he had been born on Staten Island.

In the fall of 1924, he entered Harvard University as an amiable American boy, who knew Whitman and Shakespeare, who could ride a horse and play baseball, and who cultivated a small compassionate smile that inspired trust and confidence. I can see him walking on the lawn under the brick buildings of Harvard yard with a bounce in his step. I discover him sitting under a tree, reading Cervantes, and then looking up at the sky, letting the beauty of the language and the day wash over him.

He would become fluent in Spanish, French, and Italian. In his senior year his prize-winning thesis would become a permanent part of the Harvard Library.

After college, he tackled Wall Street, becoming a broker, an actuary, and finally chief executive officer of his own credit bureau. I can envision him walking the narrow streets of downtown Manhattan in a fitted gray suit, the buildings on either side of him as tall and imposing as his image of himself. I follow him to the East

River, where he feels the romance of success as a cool breeze over the water.

When the war called, he joined the army, rising quickly from lieutenant to major. I discover a picture of him grinning under his major's cap, holding a bulky parcel in one hand and a sign that says 'Post Exchange Main Store' in the other. He is showing off his territory.

My mother, a green-eyed beauty who captivated him with her charm, became part of his domain as wife and mother. She was twenty-five, and he was forty-three. Her glamour evoked a rage in him as well as a pride. Would she stride away from him never to return? In the bulky frame of the man he had become, the small-frightened boy of his childhood re-emerged. He wanted to wound his wife with criticism and disapproving silences the way his father had wounded him. "You're all surface and no substance," he would say with a solemn and disappointed expression. How could he protect her when there was a part of him that couldn't protect himself?

My earliest memory of my father was when I was about aged three or four. He was lifting me by the arms and swinging me back and forth in front of a wide picture window in our house on the New Jersey shore. "Swing me," I shouted. "Daddy swing me." Later in the day, he planted tomatoes in our garden, lying on his stomach, his solid frame becoming one with the earth. In the evening, he filled the house with operatic music and taught me the libretto of Madam Butterfly.

My father in his Major's uniform, circa 1943

When my mother left him, hope and youth and the joy of achievement left too. He had lost his job and his zest for life. I remember visiting him in his small hotel room on Manhattan's Upper West Side, where there were half-eaten Three Musketeers bars on the dresser and a dirty gray carpet. He sat on his bed, looking bent and forlorn, regarding me as if I were a stranger instead of his twelve-year-old daughter.

As the years passed, he became appalled at my neglecting to comfort him when he was unemployed and alone. An angry tremble had crept into his voice. His comments seemed designed to whittle away at my self-esteem. "I don't know how a daughter of mine could be so slow minded," he said. "Life gets more and more miserable every day, doesn't it, Steph?"

When I was nineteen, he developed a rare blood disease and lay bleeding internally in a Boston hospital. I remember his matted brown hair, the needle in his arm for a transfusion, and the mystified expression on his face. How had his life come to this? There was an aura of hopelessness about him that made me want to escape. Even his devoted new wife couldn't lift his spirits. When the doctor said there was no imminent danger, I made travel plans. His wife perceived this decision as a monumental lack of concern, which sent her into a rage; she charged at me physically, and I grabbed her thin white wrists. "You're a selfish, rotten girl," she said.

"I guess I struck out when I had a daughter," my father murmured.

I stormed out of the hospital full of righteous indignation, secretly believing that they were right about me, and determining never to see them again.

Five years later a remembered tenderness for my father caused my resolve to weaken. For the next fifteen years, we would meet for lunch in his cheerless Manhattan office in the check-signing division of a department store. It is here that he would rhapsodize about Harvard and the senior thesis that had so engaged his interest. At eighty-two he had a vision of forming a financial conglomerate in India. Two years later he would die quietly in his sleep.

Annette from Gloversville

After my father died, my stepmother didn't smack the plates on the table quite so hard when she asked me to dinner. A bubble of distrust seemed to have broken between us. I remember one evening dining with her on her stone terrace overlooking the city. There were peach trees around us and boxes with colorful flowers that my father had planted. She served curried chicken and a salad flavored with Indian spices.

We spoke of daily things, my job and hers. She told me about her class, where Chinese students brought candy wrapped in red paper, and how they made a shrine for her when her husband died and said a prayer. We didn't discuss the history of tension between us, nor the time when she and my father were having their picture taken at a New Jersey fair, and she had asked me not to be in it. With my father gone we enjoyed a fresh current of air.

She began taking me as her guest to the Museum of Modern Art, where we would wander easily through the halls checking out Van Goghs and Gauguins, and trying to decipher the patterns of lines in Jackson Pollock's paintings.

In spring, when the weather was warm, we would sit in the sculpture garden, facing a fountain. It was there that she would tell me about growing up in Gloversville, New York in a white house with cracked green shutters and a lawn in front of it, where she and her sister, Sylvia, played like tomboys; she told me about her quiet father and effusive mother, who never quite approved of anything she did or said. She let me know she was the first woman glove inspector in Albany, New York. She spoke of her passion for travel and how she had been to Asia and Africa. She recalled a time when flying over India, the pilot had invited her into the cockpit and let her steer the plane. She reminded me of how stubborn my father was and how kind he could be.

Her cancer diagnosis came suddenly; cells traveled throughout her body like a moving train. I sat in the hospital with her, watching her small face on the pillow and her bright blue eyes watching me. I stroked her thin cheek. I was there when her breath stopped. Love was in the room although we never called it that.

Aunt Aida's Kitchen

My aunt Aida invited me to dinner in her Florida apartment. It had pristine white sofas and beige carpeting. She served dinner in her kitchen at six o'clock on a summer evening. The sun came in like a glass of lemonade poured over the white Formica table. Around us there were shelves lined with spices, green hanging plants, and family pictures in Lucite frames. One picture was a faded image taken in Newark in the 1930's of her parents, Sonia and Joseph with their children, Rose and Phil and Nathan, all three of whom had died young of heart failure, and aunt Aida and my mother, who were the only living family members.

Aunt Aida was fastidious. The table was set with plastic mats and decorated with fresh flowers in a plastic vase. We ate tender chicken and green beans and soft mashed potatoes with butter. I was thirty-nine and she was a mysterious age called 'old'; lines made a rumpled quilt across her face. "It's so nice to see you," she said. Her blue eyes had a playful light in them.

We pressed hands and smiled at each other. Her smile was much sweeter than the one I had seen in pictures when she was a young woman in a low cut black dress with her head tossed back; she was married to her second husband, Ben, who had small blue eyes and an immense stomach. Her first husband, Dave, who was lean and nimble, sneaked off with his mistress, who for years he pretended was a second job in Philadelphia.

Shortly before Aunt Aida turned fifty, she was walking across a hilly street in Elizabeth, New Jersey when a wayward truck without brakes knocked her over and ripped off her right leg, almost taking her life. She recovered and learned to carry herself easily and gracefully on a plastic prosthesis with only the hint of a limp.

When Aunt Aida got up to get us some chocolate ice cream, she noticed me watching her and said when she sat down again, "People thought I didn't cry after the accident, but I did. I cried every night. Finally I said to myself, 'The leg is missing. What am I going to do now?'"

The answer included managing an office, keeping meticulous house, becoming a wizard at Mahjong, and driving like a cowboy along the roads and highways of New Jersey and Florida.

A month after our dinner, while driving her Camry along Indian Creek, which was sparkling in sunlight, her heart stopped at a traffic light.

PART V

Coming to Terms

Without Warning

On a cold day in March just before dusk I walk down Fifth Avenue across the street from Central Park opposite the Metropolitan Museum. Pink afternoon light casts a spell across the sky. The people in the park move in a stream. I am gliding with them. Hatless, I feel the wind lift my long, dark hair. At thirty-nine I am committed to youth, to the alacrity of movement, to my buoyant steps and straight spine. I toss back my head and smile. Time can't touch me. I shiver. The chill transforms into a band of sweat around my neck and then settles as a heat against my chest. I throw open my coat and breath deeply. This sensation leaves as imperceptibly as it came.

In the weeks and months that follow I awaken in the night aware of the same faint collar of perspiration. Vigilant and alert, my mind seems capable of observing my body as if they were separate entities. My period loses its rhythm. I am no longer ruled by the gravitational pull of the moon. The monthly flow of blood that has carried away my darkening moods is replaced by a bimonthly trickle.

My gynecologist, a serious young woman with illustrious credentials, is concerned and schedules an endometrial biopsy. "This is just a precautionary measure," she says reassuringly. I submit to the scraping of my uterus. Pain rips through me like an electric current. I am too stunned to cry out. While the test reveals normal cells, I am not ovulating. "Let's wait and see," she says cautiously. Meanwhile my periods have resumed their flow. My body temperature has regulated itself. I pronounce myself well.

That summer in Italy in the merciless heat of Pompeii, I begin to bleed profusely, running in shame to my hotel room to wash my clothes. The heavy flow ceases as suddenly as it began and becomes a normal period. I am furious at my body's rebelliousness. Once back in New York, I re-experience cycles of heat and cold at unexpected moments. While hormone irregularities have appeared in my twenties and thirties, playing havoc with my period, I sense something more poignant is at work here. For two months my period stops altogether. I recall stories of my grandmother who lost a kidney giving birth at thirty-six to a change-of-life child, my mother. I remember my mother entering menopause in her mid-thirties. Suspicion becomes a certainty that I pick up and discard. *I am a young woman after all. This can't be happening to me.* My erratic periods and body temperature tell me differently. I ask my doctor to test for menopause.

She is skeptical about my diagnosis. "Women regardless of genetics menstruate longer in this generation," she explains. "You're more active and health-conscious than your grandmother." An examination corroborates her opinion. She smiles down at me. "You're skin is soft. Your vaginal tissues are moist. You are not a woman entering menopause."

I sit on her table in a thin white paper coat, letting her words provide a balm. I am aware of my slender body under the coat, the youthful encasement that has always been mine, and I don't want to relinquish. "Please do the test," I say. "I'll feel better knowing for sure."

She concedes graciously. As she draws blood, she shares her medical knowledge with me. "If your follicle stimulating hormone, the FSH serum level, is high, then your ovaries are losing their capacity to produce eggs."

Losing *their capacity*. The words threaten to ensnare and define me. I cast them away. A few days later my normal period resurfaces; hope stirs as a purring in my chest. When her call comes, we are both surprised by the results.

"You are well into the menopausal cycle," she tells me. Her tone is gentle, regretful. "An early loss of estrogen can pose health risks for a woman your age. There is a possibility of osteoporosis and heart disease. You have to start taking hormone replacement therapy immediately."

Caught in a tunnel of diminishing options, I can barely breathe. "I need to think about this," I say. "I can't talk now."

Stalking the circumference of my small Manhattan apartment, I try to outdistance the news. Outside it is winter again. The cold blue air feels as unrecognizable to me as I do to myself. Without an ideology for aging, I don't know who I am. I am not ready to make a decision about estrogen. When I tell close friends what is happening to me, I feel as if I'm talking about someone else.

At home I study my face in the dusty antique mirror above my dresser. The lines around my mouth seem more apparent and my cheeks have a pinched and tired look; my skin appears sallow. A wave of sadness swells inside me thicker than blood and darker than the winter night. I cry for the loss of my youth with a deep heaving sound.

Tears cleanse and help me to remember myself as a girl of thirteen, exuberant at the first sight of her period. *She pulls her robe open in front of a full length mirror, admiring the curve of her breasts and hips, the woman's body that is newly hers and now bleeds monthly. In celebration of this gift, she skates wildly across a frozen lake: blood is power and immortality. I follow the rising tide of her sexuality into her twenties and thirties, fueled by the ebb and flow of blood. I see the lovers that have left her and she has left. I envision the children she might have had thriving in the bloody warmth of her womb. I feel the energy that courses through her in the absence of blood and youth, the power of her body and soul to stride alone into an uncertain future.*

There is not a specific instance in time when I come to accept the menopausal transition, but rather a compilation of moments that bring me closer to my changing self. I pull my hair back into a braid and then cut it short when I notice it shedding on my pillow. An eerie tingling sensation comes into my fingers. I read voraciously on the subject of menopause and attend conferences on women's health. When a bone density test shows loss at my left hip, I take a natural form of estrogen and progesterone. I sleep more soundly and my hair stops falling out. At work I begin to talk, even joke, about menopause. When I notice a young woman eyeing me cautiously, I smile at her and say, "It's not catching."

After making sporadic visits over the next four years, my period stops, and I achieve an emotional stasis that I never knew while menstruating. My sexuality is a gentler stirring of pleasure. I have become more sensitized to the natural world, and I am more prone to taking risks, asking myself the questions, *If not now when?* On a plane trip south, I allow myself the sensation of skydiving.

More than a decade has passed since I began the menopausal passage. Snow is blanketing the ground as I walk up Fifth Avenue. My body feels strong in the folds of my coat. My steps are attuned to the rhythm of the night.

Visiting Keats's Urn

At forty-five I decide to revisit the poem I revered most in high school, Keats' *Ode on a Grecian Urn*. I discover the same delicately painted images on the urn—trees in springtime, young lovers beneath a tree, a deserted seaside town whose citizens have gathered for the sacrifice of a heifer adorned in garlands. The poet's words wrap me in a cadence of silent music. "Thou still unravish'd bride of quietness! Thou foster-child of silence and slow time… Not to the sensual ear but more endear'd/Pipe to the spirit ditties of no tone."

I imagine entering the poem's mysterious present. I listen intently as the poet addresses the natural world. "Ah happy, happy, boughs! That cannot shed /Your leaves, nor ever bid the Spring adieu." He speaks to the lovers beneath the tree: "Bold lover, never, never, canst thou kiss, /Though winning near the goal." I feel the sway of their lust and am reassured by the poet's words … "do not grieve;/ For ever wilt thou love, and she be fair!"

Questions vibrate like musical notes. Along with Keats I wonder, "What men or gods are these? What maidens loath? What leaf-fringed legend haunts about thy shape?" I have become the sacrificial heifer "lowing at the skies" of uncertainty.

I enter a town by the sea where mountains cast a shadow above empty streets so still the soul can come in. Doubts fall away as I touch the infinite without the weight of reflection. "Thou, silent form, dost tease us out of thought/As doth eternity." I feel truth crystallize as a moment of beauty. "'Beauty is truth, truth beauty,' – that is all/Ye know on earth, and all ye need to know."

The Eternal Now

I am always late. Late for attendance in the moment as if I am watching myself watch the stars. Will I remember the sky pressing down on my head or the musty crescent moon or the pink clouds streaking into darkness? I am describing the moment as if I weren't there, a document of a life half-lived as I watch myself watching my world. What if the present were chronicled as the past so the moment had no real life of its own, and the baby rabbit I see munching on grass were already a memory? What is this present I am always late for? What would happen if I showed up for it? Would it be too painfully beautiful, too real? Would the sky explode? Is it too risky to let life happen moment by moment? Will skipping over the present avert disaster?

In a moment I fully inhabit I hear chimes, I feel the wind, a motor hums; birds sing and stop. I hear a rake, a hammer, and a whistle. I see wild flowers that are red and orange and yellow. I watch them bend unselfconsciously. I see a pile of wood and a tall tree with a puzzle of tiny leaves. I see rocks on a table and a giant sand-colored five-point star nailed to the gray bricks of a New

England house. I see white lace curtains on a rectangular window. I see a profusion of blue flowers, fists of delicate petals. I see perfectly clear sky and giant trees, dangerous green leaves against the blue, trembling and then almost still. I see a chimney made of Flemish brick. There! Was that so difficult?

My Mother Never Told Me

My mother never told me where her rage came from. I watched the blood beat at her temples and her mouth tighten into a grimace. I listened to the piercing sound of her voice. I watched her run past moving cars as if propelled by lightning. My mother told me some things—that the enemy was everywhere, and that storm clouds were always gathering.

I imagine her at eight, wandering down a street in Newark, New Jersey, her chin pointed at the sky. Her dark hair is cropped close to her head; she is a dot in brown overalls and a starched white blouse. Not her mother, nor her father, nor her two sisters and two brothers know she is gone. She runs as if her feet could thud out a song of belonging. She runs past houses with white shutters and stiff flowers that don't share their fragrance. She runs so that her heart won't stop beating. She is alive though no one can see her.

When my mother was ten, her appendix burst. Poisonous juices ran loose in her belly. She was rushed to the hospital with sirens blaring and a block of fear in her chest. Her mother refused to go with her because it was the Sabbath. God came before her daughter.

I can imagine my mother awakening from the anesthetic to the smell of alcohol and sweat. She is too angry and frightened to cry. No one, no one can be counted on.

My mother didn't remember much about her childhood. She did remember the wind and the rain on the day her mother died and the foyer clock beating out time as if it could turn back, making her own mother young again with a pale white face, saying to her, "Gertrude, I love you. You are my star."

★ ★ ★

My mother was comfortable with fire. She liked the feel of a match, striking raw and hard in her hand. She could spit flames. Hard dark ash. Conflagrations of hatred. "I am only hitting back," she would explain.

She sought freedom from anyone who might hold her down, defy, or betray her. In the last years of her life, she would drive past palm trees and waterways in Miami Beach, letting the flat pavement unfold beneath her; she loved the thud of the wheels and the hum of the engine, allowing her to pump speed. She drove endlessly as if stopping were a glitch in her life plan; it implied memory, pain, and regret.

My mother never told me where her rage came from—wagging a finger at me on her deathbed, her words, fading into incoherent breaths as if this final rasp of air were a claw digging into the unfair center of her world.

Now three years have passed. *Her voice comes to me in dreams. Don't accuse me. Listen to what I have to say. I have compassion for you, for my own mother, for nations at war, for a world that can't live without shields and disguises. It's the softness that the world destroys, the softness we are forced to hide.*

What Did I have To Lose?

I never intended to take care of my mother. She lived in Miami by the sea; I lived under the steel, glass, and brick structures of Manhattan. For twenty years I limited our contact to terse semiannual visits.

"Don't count on me when you get old," I would tell her.

And then the cancer began to eat away at her. On my now frequent visits, we would lie back on adjacent beds, watching reruns of Matlock on television. Giving the screen our rapt attention, we followed dated stories of deceit and justice. Andy Griffith, cast as a silver haired attorney, scratched his head in mild-mannered dismay just before he cracked a particularly difficult case. Murderers were always brought to justice. Much of the action took place in Matlock's house, which he shared with his jovial and attractive daughter, a woman in her thirties, who worked with him. We loved listening to their slow Middle American drawl as they sat around the kitchen table with its starched white cloth. While they often chided one another, their love was evident. Matlock was our balance wheel in this season of death, the good parent we never had.

"I look like a skeleton," my mother would say. "I'm so ugly."

"No," I'd say and shake my head. And think but not say, *You look like a child, so gaunt and shiny as if your eyes could record all the hurt and beauty in the world.*

What did her cruelty matter—words that sliced like knives through decades? What did I have to lose by loving her?

Running out of Gas

All that rage that I held pent up and gray like lava exploding even across worlds. I savored hating you. You were robust in your cruelty, a magnificent beast that could growl like a diesel truck releasing fumes in my face. I see the cloud resettling and being consumed by rain. I am running out of steam, gas, and incentive for lashing back at you. Hate, I suspect, was the mask you wore, a shield against fear. I find myself assaulting a water bug in my city apartment, dousing it with spray, smacking it with the hard back of a Webster's dictionary, and I realize you thought I was your enemy.

Mother, who are you now? Have you coalesced with the sky? Are you light as rain? Has death given you a new passageway into light where brilliant colors rest on hilltops and the sky is always as soft as a meadow? Do you read books in the open air? Do you design dresses that have elegant simple lines and slide on like skin? I hear your voice in my ear quiet as roses, "Love yourself."

Where has my hatred gone? Let it rise up and join with the stars. I am running out of gas so that I may turn onto a broader road, where the pavement is as soft as sorrow and as light.

Sacred Lotuses 2007

Decisions

For Linda Wilhelm and Samantha Wilhelm

My friend, Linda, and her daughter, Samantha, invite me to a restaurant in Chelsea, where jazz is being played. The lights are dim and the music has surprising and unexpected riffs that meander into a discordant terrain. I am not sure I like it. I can't escape the beat or lose myself in it; the sound requires my undivided attention.

Samantha, who at sixteen has dyed her hair a magnetic shade of pink, greets me with a gentle smile; she is here doing research for a class project on jazz. After the first set her mother calls over the drummer, a man named Bob with a gray ponytail and intense blue eyes, who tells us that the music he loves originated in Africa and has improvisation at its heart; he and his fellow musicians can embellish and invent melody as they go along.

When Bob returns to his drums, Linda flashes a brilliant smile. It is at her suggestion that I am here tonight, sharing in their adventure. Linda and I have had a long-standing controversy over the validity of genetic determinism; she contends that our temperaments are encoded in our genes and is heartened by the fact that her father's

DNA is guaranteeing her happiness. Nothing ruffles her equanimity, not even my raging disagreement with her. I am an ardent believer in free will. I have to be. I come from a line of cynics; disagreeable words came off their tongues and settled under them; they took pride in being enraged and disgruntled.

I see an image of my mother, sitting in the kitchen, dressed in a rumpled pink nightgown. "People are always suffering," she says. "All day. All of the time." I see my father's furrowed brow and the deep circles of disappointment under his eyes. When my mother left him, his hope, youth and courage went with her. "Everyone is out to get me," he says.

My genetic makeup rises up and mocks me. How can I hope to escape it if not by deciding to think bright thoughts? Yet my predilection for worry is a stubborn enemy of optimism. My resolve is tested daily by the leaks in my apartment, the delays on the subway and the niggling feeling that my sense of good health is a balloon that could burst at any moment.

At my yearly mammography, I wait for the results in a windowless room with flowered wallpaper and a steel sink. Hope, I realize, is the torch I must burn in the face of uncertainty. A technician with an impassive face comes in and says, "You're okay." I feel every part of me smile.

Yet angst comes again in the weeks that follow. What of next year's mammography, the atrocities of war and natural disasters, and of course my own personal discontents?

I think of my friend, Sharyn, scaling a precipitous mountain in

Burma. Once at the top, the ancient city unfolded beneath her. "Weren't you afraid?" I asked. She shook her head. "I just concentrated on each step."

I think of my friend, Enid, going off to brain surgery with a sanguine smile on her face. She presses my hand, utterly attuned to the moment of friendship.

My mind wants to zoom back to missed opportunities and agonize over future possibilities; the now often gets lost in the ruckus.

As if intuiting my thoughts, Linda reaches over and takes one of my hands and her daughter, Samantha, the other. I decide to enter the circle of good feeling. I close my eyes. The music sounds like jangling bells and then begins to jump and spin and swell into a caravan of joining rhythms, the only sounds there are.

Walk With My Father

Often in my dreams I hear my father singing; his voice has a lilt to it, a little trembling sound. I imagine it was a melody he invented during his youth on the Lower Eat Side. I see him walking down the street, taking long purposeful strides. It is summer and the heat comes up from the asphalt like steam. At fourteen, my father has his hands in his pockets; he whistles through his full lips a tune of his own invention, a melody full of all the things he can do.

He turns down Great Jones Street, which is bustling and alive and thick with people. Girls in faded brown shawls are hovering together, sending up a buzz of talk in Yiddish and English. He would love to stop and join them but doesn't allow himself the distraction. He is headed for Mr. Kruger's classroom in a dark building with stairs that creak and windows that are covered with dust, making the outside seem like a dream. Mr. Kruger will administer a test that if he passes will allow him entry into a school for gifted kids.

Just last night his mother had pinched his arm and said, "Louie, you are the chosen one in the family." The pressure of her thumb made her words seem true; he could climb the ladder of her dreams and his. But what if he fell, tumbling like his brother to the bottom of the class? He, Louie, the runt of the litter disguised as a king.

As he enters a dark building and begins to climb the stairs, he feels his stomach tremble with each step. The classroom has a dark hazy light as if the air were a brown mist coming up around him. He can hear the rustling of pushcarts on the street below and a man hollering "Ices!" and a shout that sounds almost like a cannon.

Suddenly he is in another time and place. Gunfire sings in the air. A man in a gray tunic grabs him by the arm and shoves him into the mud-covered corner of his home in Odessa. He feels the pressure of a boot against his chest and wants to shout, "Mama," but he can't find the sound. He is five; his breath is almost still. His small brown eyes are looking for light in the darkness. He hears the man's footsteps receding on the floorboards, the way his own feet sounded ascending the stairs. Yet today the cranking, moaning sound will take him to victory. He sees himself standing apart from the dirt and the heat, from the parched air and the amoeba-like crowds of the Lower East Side. He is going places.

Mr. Kruger, a man with short red hair and a matching mustache and an ill-fitting jacket ushers my father into the classroom, where he finds boys like himself sitting at small brown desks with inkwells and pens and test books waiting for them. He imagines himself dipping his pen inside one of the inkwells, marking each answer correctly, scoring perfectly in math and science and reading.

When the test begins, my father moves his pen fearlessly across the page. Light seems to hum inside him and around him as he finishes and waits triumphantly for the others to catch up.

At the desk next to him, a boy named Saul, a prankster with mischievous blue eyes and a stick-thin leg due to polio, reaches over and makes a parody of grabbing for my father's test. My father shoves him away with a harsh protective gesture. Mr. Kruger almost runs down the aisle; his mustache seems to stand apart from his face. He pulls both boys up by the scruff of their necks. "You're disqualified," he says in a fierce whisper. "Come back next year when you can behave like young men should."

Back down on the street my father's anger feels hotter than the summer air. Saul punches his arm playfully and flashes a crooked smile. "Hey, Louie, I was only kidding around. Honest."

My father's rage feels like a wire about to snap; he stands so close to Saul, he can see his own reflection in the other boy's eyes. Saul, who cares only about the sway of girls' breasts under their thin blouses. Saul who rode the Third Avenue El with Leila Beckman to a place where they could lie on the grass, and he could place a hand on her thigh. Saul, who although he is smart, doesn't care if he ever amounts to anything, has ruined his life. My father hears himself shout in a voice so loud it seems to grab hold of the sky. "Don't you ever, ever do anything like that again. Do you hear me?"

As Saul limps away, my father sits down on the stoop. His anger has wilted in the heat and a small tired feeling replaces it, which soon turns to fear. He wraps his arms around his chest. What will his mother say when he tells her what has happened? He can feel

Coming to Terms

the weight of her disappointment pressing down on him.

★ ★ ★

Shortly before his death my father and I attended an opera together. It was winter; he took off his coat, folded it neatly, and placed it beneath his seat. Then he folded his arms across his chest in a tight little gesture, looking straight ahead, waiting for the music to start. I imagine reaching over and touching his hand and saying, "You're fine just the way you are." And he smiles, showing small white teeth, like mine.

Saying Goodbye

My mother never said goodbye to me. Oh, I was there the day she died behind the stained glass door to her bedroom. "Come over here," she said. And I came to her and put my arms around her.

"You're suffering," she said.

"I'm fine," I said.

Our painful history spun in the air between us.

My mother believed the astral plane was a quick step up a ladder of light. Once she was gone, the thought of her watching me eternally made me want to throw a cloak over my head. She glared at me from picture frames; she scorned the dust on my floor and the chaos in my mind. It took me almost five years to realize that I was keeping her voice alive.

So many memories. I am eight years old. My mother and I are standing on a red, carpeted staircase leading up to her Manhattan apartment. She has given me a bag of peaches to carry. "Stand up straight," she scoffs. "You look like a cripple." I let the peaches fall and tumble down the stairs. "I'll make you pay for this," she shouts. Tiny points of fear ripple inside me.

My mother, 1967

I lie in a bed in another of my mother's Manhattan apartments, fighting a fever brought on by hepatitis. Having taken on the challenge of nursing me, she brings me fragrant soups and bread so fresh it reminds me of spring air. She pulls up a chair and sits by my bedside. I am amazed by the depth of tenderness in her face.

My mother never told me goodbye, so I will have to say goodbye to her. She rises up before me in a white satin dress; her eyes shine with initiative; she is not the gentle mother that I had dreamed of having; she is a strong woman. The day she died she said, "You can have the newspaper tomorrow. I won't be needing it." I watched her meet death with grace and astounding courage, and it is how I will remember her.

Airports

In the summer of 1966, a widespread airline strike grounds planes across America. My mother, my stepfather, and I have first class tickets traveling east from Los Angeles to Kennedy Airport in New York on one of the few remaining carriers. They are sitting in front of me, and I have two luxurious seats for myself until a man in a red bowtie and a classy sports jacket slips into the window seat beside me. His hair is pulled tightly across his head in a fine brown net; his long nose curves like a slide. I recognize him immediately as Bob Hope, the iconic comedian and actor, who has graced my television set since childhood. At sixteen, I am far too timid to talk to him. I lower my eyes.

My mother turns around and treats him to a magnanimous smile. She introduces herself as well as my stepfather and me and tells Bob Hope how much she admires his work and what an honor it is to meet him. Less impressed with celebrity, my stepfather offers a gruff hello and returns to his newspaper. Bob Hope thanks my mother warmly and politely. The plane begins to race across the runway and rise effortlessly.

When lunch is served, my mother turns to Bob Hope again and praises him for entertaining the troops in Vietnam. "It's amazing what you've done for their morale," she says.

"It is my proudest accomplishment," he tells her.

A few hours into the flight, the sky turns to night. The air is so calm I am unaware of the plane moving. A stewardess in a pink skirt and vest comes over and speaks to Bob Hope in a hushed voice. There is something disturbing about the click of her heels and the tight lines of her face. About a half an hour later she comes back again.

"I hope we land on time," Bob Hope says. "I have press waiting for me."

This time her voice has a nervous edge. Her teased blond hair doesn't move. Perhaps she thinks Bob Hope's fame entitles him to information other passengers won't receive. "Let's be happy if we land at all," she says. "We've lost visibility."

Seconds later the captain's voice comes over the loudspeaker. He tells us that we may attempt a landing in Boston or Philadelphia. He will keep us posted.

Silence echoes like a roar on the plane. The cabin is almost dark, and I see nothing but black sky out the window. My breath feels as tight as the air around me. I turn to Bob Hope and say, "What's going to happen?"

He laughs and his voice sounds like the one I've heard so many times on television. "Don't worry, honey. If things get rough, you can get on my back, and we'll fly out the window."

My mother turns around and our eyes meet in a kind of horror we don't name.

We all face forward as the plane hovers in the night sky. I am aware of an icy fear in my chest and the steel cage of the aircraft around me. We wait in motionless darkness. I won't let myself think about a fiery crash, splintering us all into filaments of air, taking my young life. A wave of determination comes over me; I will pit my will against the elements of fate and make sure we survive; then fear comes again. Seconds feel like hours.

At the window a bright light begins to flash like a shooting star. We smack down hard on the tarmac of a freight field at Kennedy Airport. Because of the air strike, we have the luck of not colliding with another carrier. The plane races and roars and finally pulls to a stop. The lights come on.

"I've never been through anything like this," Bob Hope says. "Even in crates over Nam."

As we walk down the ladder to the airfield, we see ambulances waiting for us, prepared for a crash landing. Reporters swarm around Bob Hope as my mother, my stepfather, and I enter the airport and head for the luggage carousel.

There is a bounce to my step. The ground feels rich with possibilities. I am alive. I feel as if my life is just beginning. I can do something extraordinary. Each time I walk through an airport, especially after a turbulent flight, I get the same feeling.